To Grand   s of
love f   naries
Christmas 84

ROYAL
HOMES
of the United Kingdom

The West front of Hampton Court Palace showing the Great Gatehouse. The oriel windows carry the arms of Henry VIII, who received the Palace as a gift from Cardinal Wolsey. The Palace soon became the honeymoon home for the monarch and his succession of wives. Edward VI, who succeeded him, was born at Hampton Court and it was here also that Catherine Howard was arrested.

ROYAL HOMES
of the United Kingdom

Neville Williams

OMEGA BOOKS

For Julia

This edition published 1983 by Omega Books Ltd,
1 West Street, Ware, Hertfordshire, under licence
from the proprietor.

Copyright © 1971 Neville Williams

ISBN 0 907853 56 0

Printed and bound in Hong Kong by South China Printing Co.

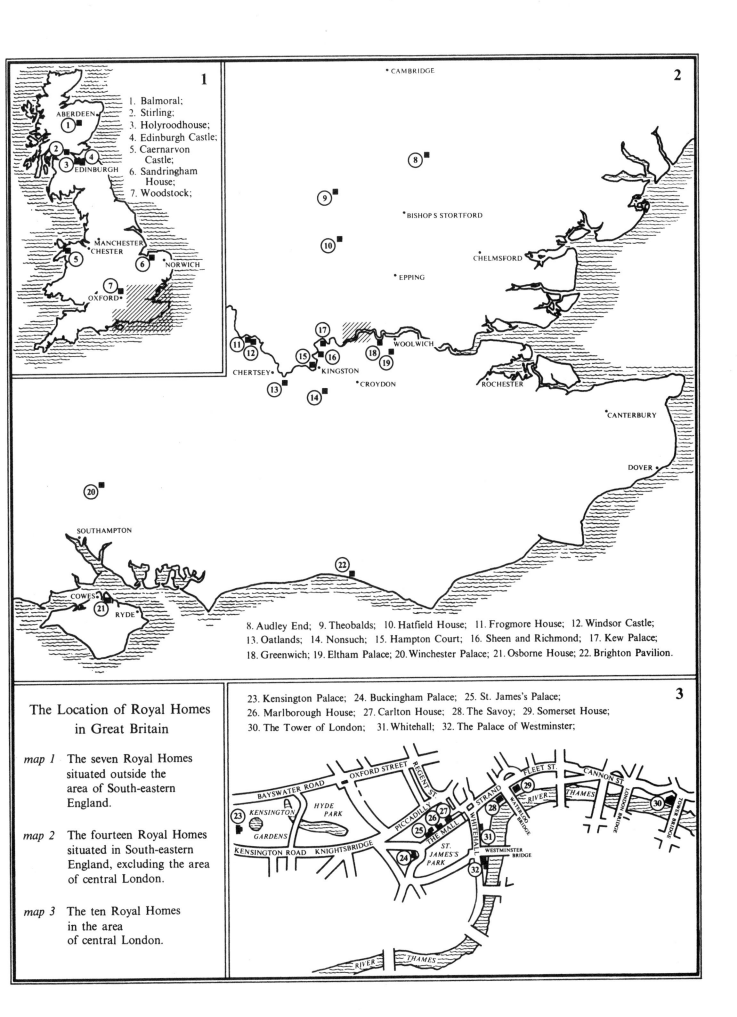

1

1. Balmoral;
2. Stirling;
3. Holyroodhouse;
4. Edinburgh Castle;
5. Caernarvon Castle;
6. Sandringham House;
7. Woodstock;

2

8. Audley End; 9. Theobalds; 10. Hatfield House; 11. Frogmore House; 12. Windsor Castle;
13. Oatlands; 14. Nonsuch; 15. Hampton Court; 16. Sheen and Richmond; 17. Kew Palace;
18. Greenwich; 19. Eltham Palace; 20. Winchester Palace; 21. Osborne House; 22. Brighton Pavilion.

The Location of Royal Homes in Great Britain

map 1   The seven Royal Homes situated outside the area of South-eastern England.

map 2   The fourteen Royal Homes situated in South-eastern England, excluding the area of central London.

map 3   The ten Royal Homes in the area of central London.

3

23. Kensington Palace; 24. Buckingham Palace; 25. St. James's Palace;
26. Marlborough House; 27. Carlton House; 28. The Savoy; 29. Somerset House;
30. The Tower of London; 31. Whitehall; 32. The Palace of Westminster;

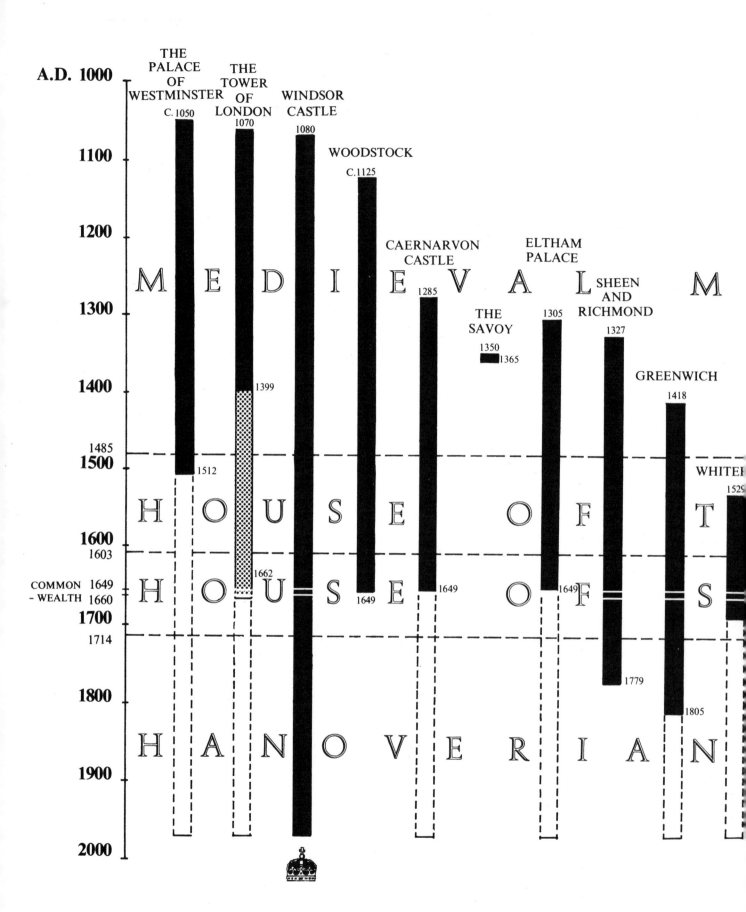

Contents

Acknowledgements

The author has benefited from the advice, so freely given, of Mr. Michael Foxell from the very first, and in the later stages has leant heavily on Mr. John Bunn and Mr. Cedric Bush. To them, and to the many others who have helped in the selection of illustrations and in the production of the book, he pays warm tribute.

The Publishers wish to acknowledge the following copyright holders for permission to use the illustrations which are here listed under the page on which they occur (the letters a, b, c, indicate the order in which they appear from top to bottom).

Aerofilms Ltd.—17, 21, 91, 105, 117, 128; Ashmolean Museum (Sutherland Collection) —65; Bodleian Library, Oxford—28b, 29; Brighton Art Collection and Museum— Jacket illustration, 111, 113, 114; British Travel Association—31b; By Gracious Permission of Her Majesty The Queen—24b, 26, 78, 102, 122; Caernarvonshire Record Office—31a, 32; Central Office of Information—12b, 49, 53, 80a & b, 84; Country Life Ltd.—35; County Seely Library, Isle of Wight—115, 116; Courtauld Institute of Art— 41b, 51, 70, 71, 108a; The Earl of Scarborough—64a & b; John R. Freeman Ltd.—20b, 37a, 48b, 68, 72, 76, 87, 88a; G. Bernard Hughes—98a; A. F. Kersting—Frontispiece, 19, 37b & c, 42, 46, 47, 54, 55b, 57, 66, 74, 77a & b, 79, 81, 88b, 93b, 103, 110, 126, 127; Keystone—90; London Museum—62, 63a & b; T. F. A. Manning, F.R.I.B.A.—38; Mansell Collection—40; Ministry of Public Buildings and Works—Half-title, 48a, 96a; National Maritime Museum—41a, 43; National Portrait Gallery—18b; Public Record Office—28a; Radio Times Hulton Picture Library—24a, 94, 118, 121, 123; Royal Institute of British Architects—14, 15, 55a, 58, 86, 92, 93a, 101a & b, 124; The Syndics of the Fitzwilliam Museum, Cambridge—60; Thomas Nelson & Sons Ltd.—7, 108b; The Trustees of the British Museum—8, 12a, 18a, 20a, 23, 52a & b, 56, 96b & c; The Trustees of the Victoria and Albert Museum—106a; Westminster City Library—33; Winchester City Museums—85.

Buckingham Palace. The 1855 Room, commemorating its occupation by Napoleon III and Empress Eugénie at that date, though the elegant furniture is principally of the Regency period.

FOR all that has vanished through fire or neglect, Britain still boasts a remarkable heritage of Royal Homes which down the centuries have been the setting for so many historical events. Stately home and ruined castle, moated manor-house and princely palace, all have continued to fascinate visitors from abroad no less than British subjects, ever since the wives of William the Conqueror's Norman Knights included a view of Edward the Confessor's Palace of Westminster in their Bayeux Tapestry. The following pages tell in text and illustration the tale of the principal houses of English and Scottish sovereigns; the manner of their foundation, their rise to importance, architectural developments at each to meet changed conditions at court and, in all but five royal houses, their ultimate fall from favour.

Her Majesty the Queen has three official residences today: Buckingham Palace, Windsor Castle and Holyroodhouse, and two private houses, Sandringham and Balmoral. These are no more, and no less, than her great grandfather, King Edward VII had, in the earliest years of this century. By Tudor standards, however, the House of Windsor is poorly served, for Queen Elizabeth I boasted fourteen

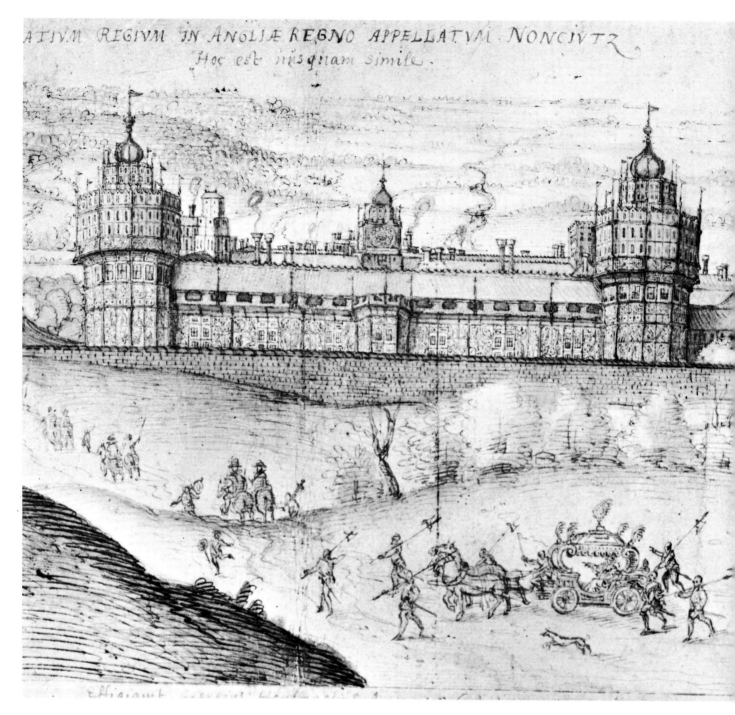

ATIVM REGIVM IN ANOLIÆ REGNO APPELLATVM NONCIVTZ
Hoc est nisquam simile.

palaces in regular use in England, yet thought herself hard done by in comparison with her medieval predecessors who owned well over a score of palaces, manors and hunting-lodges, some in or near the capital, the rest scattered about the southern and midland counties.

Fashions in localities have changed and in time have brought changes to the landscape. Tastes in architecture have altered some stately homes beyond all recognition, while other royal houses have been swallowed up in later development schemes. Only the Banqueting-House survives to remind us of the glories of old Whitehall, the largest palace in Christendom. At Eltham little remains of the extensive original

Nonsuch, as drawn by Hoffnagel in 1568. Built by Henry VIII as a hunting lodge of palatial proportions, it was at this time in the possession of the Earl of Arundel who courted the young Queen Elizabeth during her summer progress of 1559, and the Queen, whose arrival at the Palace is illustrated, stayed here frequently.

8

buildings save the Great Hall. Parliament has long ousted the sovereign from his Palace of Westminster, and kings and queens come to Richard II's hall only to lie in state. The stones of Henry I's hunting-lodge at Woodstock and of Henry VIII's pleasure dome at Nonsuch have for centuries been covered up with weeds.

But certain of these palaces have kept to this day the personality of the original builder or of a single resident. The ghost of Prinney still holds court at Brighton Pavilion; while Osborne reveals as much about Queen Victoria and the Prince Consort as the letters and journals they penned so regularly at the twin writing-desks there. The rooms at Kew embody the family life of George III and Queen Charlotte. The older part of Hampton Court still bears the unmistakable stamp of Henry VIII, the modern part that of William III and Mary. For all the changes in ownership and the alterations to the buildings the Merry Monarch is still on holiday at Audley End, and the visitor to Hatfield House cannot but think of the young Elizabeth at a vanished house across the park still on the eve of a great and glorious reign, which itself jogs the memory forward to Queen Victoria's accession day at Kensington.

This survey has been presented chronologically, with the royal homes grouped together from their original foundation in four chapters: The Medieval Monarchs; The House of Tudor; The House of Stuart; and The Hanoverians and After. Such an arrangement has fewer drawbacks than, for instance, a topographical account. Rather than sub-divide the history of a particular building into different chapters, it has been thought most convenient to deal with it as a whole from the time when it was founded; this is especially the case with Windsor Castle, which has enjoyed continuous residence over many centuries. The time-scale included in the book indicates those periods of a building's lifetime which enjoyed royal occupation, and whether these Homes are extant. The adjoining maps also show the location of the Royal Homes, with special detail of the palaces along the River Thames. On the same folding page there are lists of the English and Scottish kings and queens with their dates of birth, accession and death.

In medieval times the court was not fixed at London but progressed from palace to palace the whole year through. And each royal house, even the lesser hunting-lodges, had to provide accommodation for great numbers of attendants. Much of the administration of the country in the latter Middle Ages was still in the hands of officials of the palace, for the court of those days was equivalent to Buckingham Palace, Downing Street and Whitehall of today; and a host of magnates and civil servants as well as courtiers and domestics spent much of the year on horse-back following in the wake of the monarch as he went about his realm.

Because of poor roads this travelling from palace to palace was less easy in winter, but it still went on. The only stable period in the entire calendar was Christmas. Half the delight of the twelve days of Christmas for the household staff lay in the fact that the court was settled.

Like the Red Queen in *Through the Looking Glass*, monarchs were constantly on the move, and there were cogent reasons for this. As with any landowner with scattered possessions, it was very necessary for him to visit his estates to keep his stewards up to the mark, and as he went on his way he put into practice two very wise maxims of statecraft: he got to know his realm and he showed himself to his people. Nothing did so much to maintain the average subject's loyalty as catching sight of his monarch as he rode by; nothing did so much to clip the wings of a potentially overmighty subject than a royal progress through his neighbourhood. Hunting the red deer was the chief sport of kings, but had they confined their hunting to a single park the species would soon have become extinct. The problem of the food supply for the court demanded that there should be regular changes of residence, and hygiene, primitive though it was, reinforced this. Whatever the palace, once the monarch's stay was over the royal apartments would be scrubbed out, clean rushes put on the floor and the place made habitable, for one could never foretell how soon he might be back.

Many of the fittings for a palace went with the itinerant court. Office equipment, such as wax for the seals and skins of parchment, went on the sumpter mules, trotting behind the horses that carried various pieces of furniture for the royal apartments from which no self-respecting monarch would be separated. To the groom of the Wardrobe of Beds fell the responsibility for arranging the transport of the royal bed, with its straw mattress, its feather bed, blankets, heavy curtains and ermine coverlet. Every monarch down to Charles I took his bed with him.

Roads were not the only means of communication. Wherever possible rivers were used for transporting heavy baggage and, increasingly under the Tudors, the sovereign used the royal barge for travelling from one Thames-side palace to another. Greenwich, Westminster and Whitehall, Hampton Court and Richmond were all alongside London's river, then the great highway of southern England, and had their private landing-places. Both Eltham and Nonsuch were only four miles from the river. A trip on the river which the modern parent reserves as a special treat for his child was the quickest way of travelling from one part of greater London to another down to the end of the seventeenth century. A king could go direct by water from Greenwich to Richmond in 1500 in less time than a visitor under modern conditions could make the journey by road or rail today. Proximity to the River Thames was the chief recommendation of many of the sites chosen for royal homes.

Gradually during the later Middle Ages Westminster, close to the growing capital, became the principal royal residence; and within its precincts Parliament assembled, the courts of law sat and the largest department of state, the Exchequer, had its offices. By 1533 Whitehall Palace had taken its place as the chief seat of the sovereign, yet for another 150 years Whitehall remained no more than *primus inter pares*. It was not until after the Revolution of 1688 that the court became finally fixed. Like Westminster before it, Old Whitehall perished; and the sovereign now lived for the greater part of the year in Kensington or St. James's. Kings and queens still visited their other palaces at Windsor, Hampton Court and Kew, and some of them played truant in Hanover, but the court proper stayed put. It is during the last two centuries that Buckingham Palace has been the monarchy's principal residence.

I   *The Medieval Monarchs*

The Normans were master-builders, bringing impressive castles and cathedrals of stone to the countryside, as they penetrated the land they had conquered at Hastings. It was to match the splendour of Duke William's houses in Normandy that Edward the Confessor had built a new palace at Westminster in the last days of the old Anglo-Saxon Kingdom, which continued as the monarch's principal residence throughout the Middle Ages. The Conqueror began the Tower of London and Windsor Castle, as key fortresses to hold the country and his successors developed on these sites an increasingly intricate system of defence. As the chief sport of kings was hunting the deer of the royal forest, country houses sprang up in southern and midland England, such as Woodstock, sufficiently large to accommodate the monarch and his entourage as they rested from the chase. Edward I's conquest of Wales involved the construction of an extensive system of castles, with pride of place going to Caernarvon. In the fourteenth century, while works were in constant progress at Westminster and Windsor, the Crown looked for suitable houses within easy reach of the capital, fastening in turn on Eltham and Sheen, both fortified manor houses, set in spacious parks. By the end of the Middle Ages the English royal homes were still bleak homes, bereft of comfort, yet essentially secure; and it was left to the new monarchy of the Tudors to build lavishly.

Palace of Westminster

Parlament House the Hall the Ab

The Benedictine Abbey founded on Thorney Island, a marshy district overgrown with thorns, had come to be known as the Minster in the West of London, to distinguish it from St. Paul's. During the Danish invasions it suffered much from plundering by the Danes and lived up to its description as 'a terrible place'. King Edgar and King Canute in turn gave the community their protection, but it was Edward the Confessor who undertook the complete rebuilding of the monastery. He was so attached to Westminster that between the Abbey and the Thames he built himself a new palace which was ready for occupation long before the Minster was finished.

Though William the Conqueror set the seal on his victory at Hastings by being crowned at Westminster, he made few improvements to Edward's palace, though a view of it—the earliest surviving picture of an English royal residence—appears in the Bayeux Tapestry. It was William Rufus who left his mark at Westminster by erecting the great hall. This was to be the nucleus of a completely new palace to be built to the south, and on entering the hall to hold his first court Rufus was asked by one of his knights whether it was not too large. The King replied: 'It is not half so large as it should have been and is only a bedchamber in comparison with the palace I intend to build.' His hall is 240 feet long and $67\frac{1}{2}$ feet wide, though it was not nearly so lofty as today. Three centuries after Rufus extensive repairs were made. Richard II raised the walls to a height of 90 feet, inserted new windows and constructed the wonderful hammer-beam roof, carved in the form of angels and with his personal badge of the White Hart.

While the Norman builders were changing the face of England, Westminster Palace grew in splendour. It was during the turbulent reign of Stephen that a chapel was added to the east of the great hall dedicated to the King's patron saint, St. Stephen. To the south now stood another hall, the White Hall, which boasted glazed windows

The Palace of Westminster (top, above) *drawn by Wenceslaus Hollar in 1647, more than a century after the great fire of 1512 which had destroyed most of the medieval buildings. The illustration shows St. Stephen's chapel which was the seat of the Lower House of Parliament; the Great Hall*

(*which survives to this day*) *and is shown, surrounded by a huddle of nondescript buildings, in the engraving* (above), *of 1805; and the Abbey, to which the West Towers were added by Nicholas Hawksmoor in 1734.*

Political crises had their effect on the building, which became fortified. A Londoner speaks of the palace as an 'incomparable structure, furnished with bastions and a breastwork'. From the early twelfth century the largest department of state, the Exchequer, had offices here. The royal household itinerated with the King, Councils and Parliaments could be summoned to meet at any convenient place, but the Exchequer remained at Westminster within the palace. Here, too, the judges came to sit. Like every other feudal lord the Norman Kings held their own courts in the hall and from this household tribunal developed the judicial system of the country.

Henry III of all the medieval kings was most attached to Westminster. In grand style he told his clerk of the works that a certain new chamber in the palace must be finished by the autumn, 'though you have to hire 1,000 workmen a day'. He had the walls embellished with pictures—even the wall of the royal lavatory boasted an allegorical painting of the King being rescued by his faithful dogs from the seditions of his subjects.

Henry's *tour de force* was the Painted Chamber, 31 feet high with the floor 86 feet by 26 feet. In one gable was painted the King's personal motto, 'He who does not give what he holds does not receive what he wishes'; in the opposite gable were two large lions, face to face. The flat ceiling was painted with angels and about the room were richly coloured images of the four Evangelists. Even the window jambs carried Biblical texts. Above the King's bed was a mural depicting the Coronation of Edward the Confessor and on the opposite wall the scene of the Confessor and the Pilgrim. The other walls showed Old Testament battlepieces. By the time Henry had finished the palace sprawled over six acres. Apart from St. Stephen's there were three other chapels within the precincts, while the kitchens were the most extensive of any buildings in Europe at that time.

In 1298 occurred the first serious fire in the palace. Considering the army of retainers at court, the fact that workmen were constantly about the building and the primitive systems of heating and lighting, it is a wonder that outbreaks of fire were not more frequent. A strong wind fanned the flames and soon the greater part of the palace was ablaze. The Painted Chamber was saved, but the Hall was partly damaged. For years Westminster was uninhabitable while the work of rebuilding went slowly forward. The royal apartments were first put in order. Not until the middle of the fourteenth century was the new St. Stephen's Chapel finished, not until the end was the Hall properly repaired; the floor level was raised, a new roof, as we have noticed, provided and the towers added to the north end.

The annals of the palace in the later Middle Ages would almost amount to a comprehensive political history of England. Parliament met with increasing frequency; the courts of law were so entrenched in Westminster Hall that state banquets and other functions could no longer be held there in term time; accommodation was being commandeered in various parts of the palace for more government departments that all had their origins in the King's household. Had there been no other residence to which the royal family could retreat, the position would have been intolerable.

In February 1512 the extensive kitchens, domestic quarters and most of the royal apartments were gutted by fire; the Great Hall and Painted Chamber miraculously

Palace of Westminster

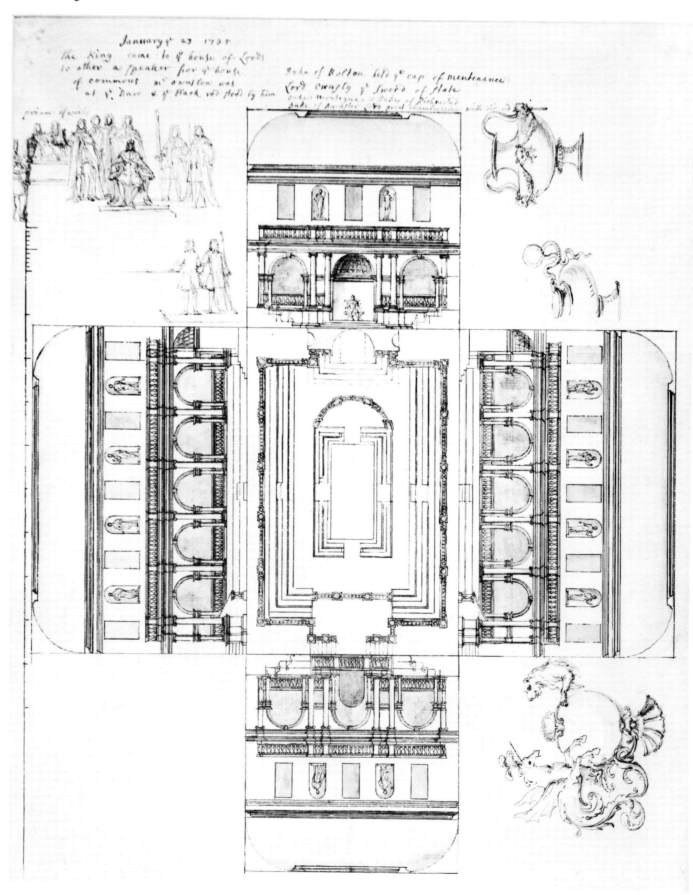

A few years after the fire of 1512 the Palace of Westminster was replaced as a royal residence by Whitehall Palace, but the name persisted, as it does to this day. By the 18th century the medieval buildings which remained and those which had been added were hardly appropriate to the dignity of Parliament and in the 1730s William Kent, the Palladian architect, prepared numerous schemes. The drawings on these pages show Kent's designs for a new House of Lords, which were never executed.

escaped. It was never rebuilt for use as a royal residence, and the fire was a turning-point in the domestic history of the sovereign.

Apart from his modest quarters in the Tower, Henry's nearest residence to the capital now was Greenwich. Desperately in need of accommodation his covetous eyes saw Cardinal Wolsey's great house at York Place, Whitehall, grow in splendour year by year, and in the end he acquired it, complete with its luxurious furnishings, and on the west side of Whitehall he founded St. James's. There was no need now to rebuild the ruins near the Abbey. State ceremonies, like the Coronation feast, were still held in Westminster, the monarch still came each year to open Parliament, but the great days of Westminster were over. Whitehall embodied the centralized New Monarchy of the Tudors and the staff of the household was completely reorganized. The destruction of the old palace 'edified before the time of mind', was almost as effective as the Reformation itself in dividing modern from medieval kingship.

Though the sovereign's own quarters had been demolished, the Great Hall, the Lesser Hall, in which Parliament met, and St. Stephen's Chapel survived. Even before the fire of 1512 further buildings had been turned over to the law. Partitions separated the portions of the Great Hall used respectively by the courts of King's Bench, Common Pleas, Chancery and Wards. State Trials were held there until 1806. The Courts finally moved to a new site at the end of the nineteenth century, and as no Coronation banquets have been held since 1821, the sole ceremonies held in the Hall

Palace of Westminster

have been the lying-in-state of monarchs and other national figures.

When the Commons began to meet separately they used the Chapter House of the Abbey until the reign of Edward VI, when the Collegiate Chapel of St. Stephen was dissolved under the second Chantries Act. The Chapel was then assigned to the Lower House which first deliberated here in 1550, and apart from the periods when St. Stephen's had been the victim of fire and bombs the Commons have met there ever since.

Apart from the Hall, little of the historic building survived the terrible fire which broke out on October 16, 1834, caused by the burning of old Exchequer tallies. They were stuffed into the furnace beneath the House of Lords, and soon the flues became red hot and the panelling in the overheated Chamber burst into flame. The strong southerly wind suddenly veered west, throwing the flames on to the House of Commons. By six o'clock next morning, when the fire was out, the Houses of Lords and Commons, the cellars from which Guy Fawkes had tried to demolish King and Parliament, the Painted Chamber, the Speaker's Lodging, the old Star Chamber and other less famous rooms were heaps of rubble. The Hall was only saved through the incomparable pluck of soldiers and firemen.

Mere restoration was out of the question, so the Parliamentary commissioners invited architects to submit their designs with 'the style to be Gothic or Elizabethan'. By November 1835 no fewer than ninety-seven entries had been submitted, of which that by Charles Barry, R.A., was selected. In the detailed drawings and their subsequent execution Barry was assisted by A. W. Pugin, who commanded an unrivalled knowledge of Gothic architecture. The first stone was laid on April 27, 1840, and by 1847 the Lords Chamber was first used, though not until 1852 were the new houses of Parliament opened by Queen Victoria. The commissioners had suggested the use of magnesium limestone from Bolsover Moor for the exterior, but it was found that the quarry could not produce the enormous quantity of stone needed and, instead, limestone from Anston, in Yorkshire, was used, though the terrace by the river was built in Aberdeen granite. For the interior Caen stone was chiefly used.

Seen from the river, Barry's New Palace of Westminster appears as a central portion with two towers, and two wings, having towers at each end. The wings and central portions are divided into thirty-five bays with hexagonal buttresses, with sunken tracery and pinnacles to each. Between the windows of each bay are exquisite carvings of the arms of sovereigns since William the Conqueror. The towers have oriel windows, and octagonal turrets at the angles. The interior is as splendid as the outside. Lobbies, entrances and corridors, no less than the great rooms of state, are embellished with painted ceilings and murals depicting notable events.

The Victorians marvelled at the statistics of 'this great temple of legislation'. The largest Gothic building in the world covered about nine acres, and comprised under its roof 15 million cubic feet. The façade on the river front was 940 feet and the tallest of the three towers, the Victoria Tower at the south-west angle, was 75-feet square and 345-feet high—dimensions which led Barry to insist that it rose by only 30-feet a year, for fear of 'settlement'. 'Compared with this magnificent altitude', wrote a contemporary, 'all the towers shrink into insignificance . . . The mind fixes

Westminster and Whitehall today, the centre of Government since Edward the Confessor sited his palace by the River Thames in 1050. In the foreground are Westminster Abbey and the Houses of Parliament (1840–65). The street of

Whitehall runs diagonally across the picture; and at the top, centre of this aerial photograph, dwarfed by Government offices, stands the Banqueting-House built by Inigo Jones in 1619–22 as part of a grandiose scheme for a new Whitehall Palace.

its massive and just proportions without distraction; and as the eye glances down its sculptured record of our line of Kings, the visitor feels that it is more than a mere tower; it is a sculptured monument of our great history as a nation.'

Not until 1859 was the great clock tower, 320 feet high, completed and installed with the clock that commemorates the name of Sir Benjamin Hall, the then Commissioner of Works; and though 'Big Ben' was left unscathed the Houses of Parliament were severely damaged in London's worst air raid on May 10, 1941.

Now that restoration in a style to harmonize with Barry's building has been completed, Parliament is planning to provide additional accommodation on the site for members of both Houses. But Westminster remains a palace, to which the sovereign usually returns in November to open a new session.

William the Conqueror's great keep, the White Tower, was a regular residence of English Kings until the end of the fourteenth century. This innermost fortress of London's castle was built to be defended. Yet once beyond the gateway through the thick walls and up the spiral staircase the White Tower was a palace in miniature. The building was entrusted by William I to a Norman monk, Gundulph, later appointed bishop of Rochester, who had stone brought over from Caen for much of the interior work, though Portland stone was used for the outer walls. The heart of the building on the first and second floors was the Chapel of St. John, a private place of worship for the royal family; retainers attended service at the Chapel of St. Peter ad Vincula. On the top floors, where an imposing collection of arms and armour is on display today, were the royal apartments. Here the steward was more important than the constable. The whitewashed walls of the banqueting chamber, privy chamber, bedrooms and council room in the centuries before tapestry hangings first gave the building the name of White Tower under Henry III.

William the Conqueror (1066–87) as depicted on a silver penny of the period.

Here in the Council Room Richard II was forced to abdicate the Crown in 1399, and in the Wakefield Tower the imbecile Henry VI was murdered in 1471 on Edward IV's instructions. The last royal tragedy at the Tower was the murder of Edward V and his brother by order of their Uncle, Richard, Duke of Gloucester, in 1483; the bodies of the Princes in the Tower were buried at the foot of the stairs.

Before the end of the Middle Ages the Tower had fulfilled its usefulness as a royal

The White Tower, which was the original keep built by William the Conqueror to maintain and proclaim his dominance over the city and its main highway, the river. It was a regular residence of English kings until the end of the 14th century and for another 250 years was used by the monarch during the Coronation ceremonies. It has been much altered since it was first built as a fortress, notably by Sir Christopher Wren in the 17th century.

residence. All over the country castles were becoming 'demobilized'. Kings no longer held their courts at Winchester or Nottingham and the castles were turned over to court rooms, judges' lodgings and prisons. With the invention of gunpowder magnates left their moated keeps for unfortified manor houses. The Tower had been built as a citadel, not as a palace and the apartments were cold, cramped and inconvenient. With more attractive buildings at their disposal at Richmond and Greenwich it is not surprising that kings and queens thought twice about climbing the difficult stairs. Perhaps it was the climb that proved too much for Henry VII's Queen, for she died in childbirth in the White Tower. Desperately short of accommodation in London after the fire at Westminster, Henry VIII put up temporary buildings in front of the White Tower to house part of his court and used rooms in the Lanthorn Tower as a Privy Chamber and bedroom. Later he began an entirely new building, the half-timbered King's House, still standing at the south-west corner which looks today much as it did in 1530. In fact Henry never lived there, for by the time it was

Tower of London

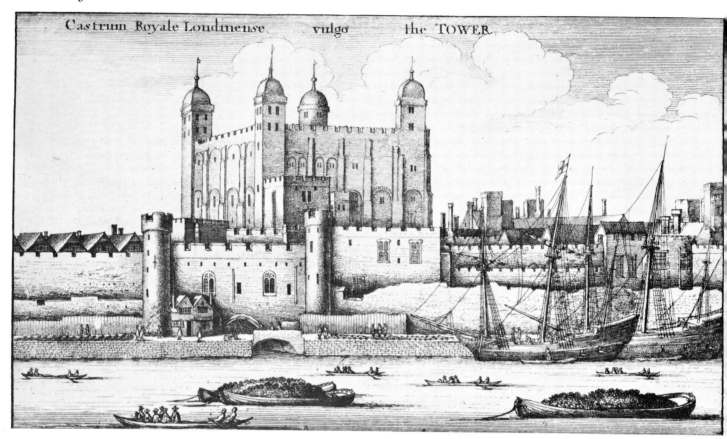

The Tower of London, drawn by Hollar in the mid-17th century. Its main approach is through the narrow tunnel from the river, known as the Traitor's Gate.

A view from Tower Hill, as seen in this painting of 1842 by Thomas Boys.

finished he had acquired Whitehall. The Privy Council met in the King's House on occasion but the building was chiefly used for important state prisoners, of whom the most eminent were Lady Jane Grey, William Penn and Rudolph Hess.

The oldest and most secure building in London, the Tower was the natural head-quarters for the Mint, the Crown jewels (even though Colonel Blood succeeded in stealing the imperial crown in 1671), the royal armoury and the national archives as well as the obvious place for prisoners of state such as Guy Fawkes, confined in 'Little Ease'; but it was not a suitable home.

There was a royal menagerie at the Tower from the time of Henry III. When he had acquired three leopards from his imperial brother-in-law, symbolic of his coat of arms, 'the Leopards of England', he decided that the Tower was the safest place for them. A camel followed and then an elephant, the gift of the King of France. A special house was constructed for the elephant and great care was taken over its food, but it died within three years and was buried within the walls. Soon the king of beasts gave his name to the Lion Tower. The menagerie was discontinued by James II.

Kings had originally taken up residence in the Tower on their accession in order to establish themselves in the great fortress commanding the capital before they had taken possession of the throne. By the later fourteenth century this Progress to the Tower by water and procession from it by road the following day had become an integral part of the Coronation festivities. The last to observe this ceremonial was Charles II and since 1661 no sovereign has spent even one night within the Tower, though St. John's chapel remains a royal chapel and the Jewel House in the Wakefield Tower is still an appendage of the palace. Of the four turrets, one is circular, and this Charles II assigned to Sir John Flamsteed, the first astronomer royal, as an observatory until Greenwich Observatory was built. Shortly afterwards Sir Christopher Wren restored the exterior of the White Tower and faced the windows of it with stone in the Italian manner.

Windsor Castle

Windsor Castle has remained a home of royalty for longer than any other building in the world, ever since William the Conqueror built the mound in 1080 as the central citadel of a great fortress that would one day cover thirteen acres. Indeed, there had been a Saxon palace by the river, three miles downstream, which was still in use until 1110. In its earliest days the Castle was no more than a Norman keep within a ditch, protected by stockades; but Henry II added many buildings, including a stone keep on the mound, and constructed both the inner moat and outer wall, with regular watch towers, to make Windsor impregnable, despite the advances in the art of siege warfare. Serious damage had been effected by siege-engines in 1189 and, again, in 1216, so Henry III strengthened the defences, especially in the Lower Ward, by constructing the western curtain wall. He also built the Curfew Tower in 1227.

The first King to adapt the fortress to a comfortable residence had been born in the Castle and until his accession as Edward III was known as Edward of Windsor. His principal architect was William of Wykeham who built a set of apartments for the King round a quadrangle in the Upper Ward of the Castle on a plan that was to become familiar at his foundations in Winchester and Oxford. It is due to him that the modern royal apartments still range round a quadrangle. He also rebuilt the Round Tower, on the Conqueror's mound, as the Devil's Tower.

A chapel dedicated to St. George, the patron saint of England, had been built in the Lower Ward of the Castle in the mid-thirteenth century, on the site of which is now the Albert Memorial Chapel. But Edward III made striking changes here on founding the Order of the Garter in 1348. The Order was to comprise the King himself, his son the Black Prince and twenty-four knights. Their spiritual welfare was to be looked after by a Dean and twenty-five canons and by twenty-six 'Poor Knights'—'decayed officers of gentle birth', who were to act as substitutes for the Garter Knights at the daily services in the Collegiate Chapel, which was enlarged, re-roofed and beautified with stained-glass windows. There were insufficient funds for completing St. George's on his ambitious plans and by 1390, when the poet Chaucer was clerk of the works, the chapel was in a sad state.

The present chapel was begun by Edward IV in 1472 and went slowly forward until the eve of the Reformation. With its delicate window tracery, flying buttresses and elaborately carved stone vaulting it is a masterpiece of Gothic architecture, a unity in itself. Long before it was completed Edward IV was buried here. For a time the Henry VII Chapel at Westminster Abbey was a rival burial place for royalty, but in the last two centuries few members of the royal family have been buried anywhere but at St. George's. Edward IV also built the Horseshoe Cloister for the canons.

Though Henry VIII rebuilt the castle gateway, few changes were made to the royal apartments in the sixteenth century, and compared with the luxury of Whitehall and Nonsuch the Castle must have seemed a bleak house. 'Methink I am in a prison',

A bird's eye view and prospect of Windsor Castle drawn by Hollar in about 1667. It clearly shows the squat Round Tower on its artificial mound, with the King's Lodgings before they were rebuilt by Charles II, (right), and St. George's Chapel (left).

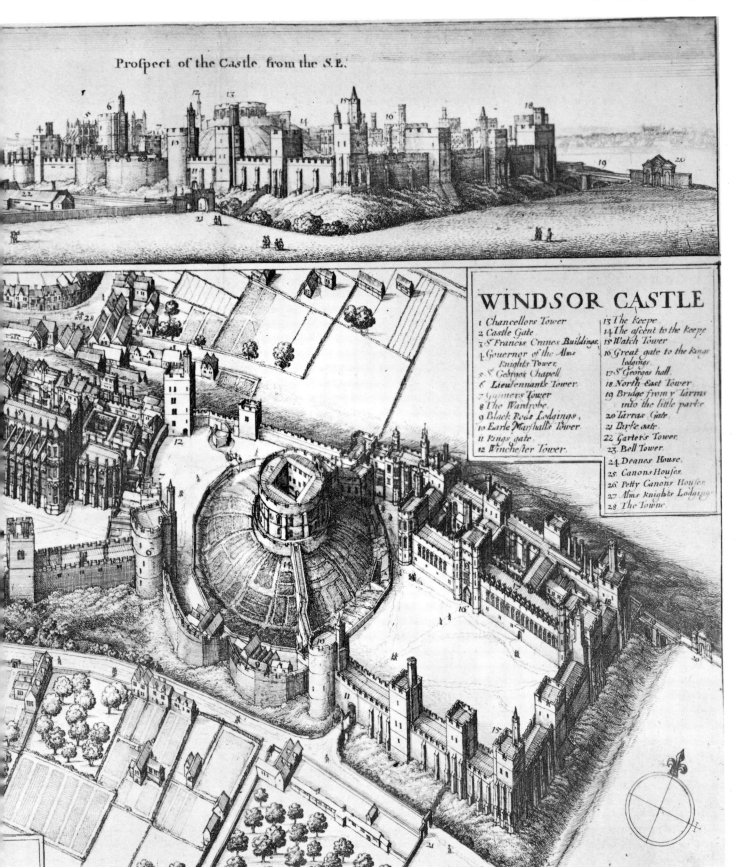

Prospect of the Castle, from the S.E.

WINDSOR CASTLE

1 Chancellors Tower
2 Castle Gate
3 St Francis Crines Buildings
4 Gouernor of the Alms Knights Tower
5 St Georges Chapell
6 Lieutennants Tower
7 Gunners Tower
8 The Wardrobe
9 Black Rods Lodgings
10 Earle Marshalls Tower
11 Kings gate
12 Winchester Tower.

13 The Keepe
14 The ascent to the keepe
15 Watch Tower
16 Great gate to the Kings lodgings
17 St Georges hall
18 North East Tower
19 Bridge from ye Tarras into the little parke
20 Tarras Gate
21 Parke gate
22 Garets Tower.
23 Bell Tower.

24 Deanes House.
25 Canons Houses.
26 Petty Canons Houses.
27 Alms knights Lodgings.
28 The Towne.

W. Hollar delineavit et sculpsit

Windsor Castle

Windsor Castle at the end of the 16th century. Queen Elizabeth I frequently resided at Windsor and it was she who built the North Terrace and a long gallery as a place in which to take exercise in bad weather.

Designs prepared in about 1824 by Jeffry Wyatt (later known as Sir Jeffry Wyatville) 'under the most ardent impression to add to the magnificence of the Castle', showing his gloomy drawings of the existing Caroline exteriors and the gothic improvements he proposed to make for George IV. Parliament were persuaded to vote £150,000 for the work which, after 16 years of continuous work, transformed the Castle at the cost of over a million pounds.

wrote young Edward VI. 'Here be no galleries nor no gardens to walk in.' His sister, Queen Elizabeth I, always regarded Windsor as the safest place in her realm and in moments of crisis would repair here 'knowing it could stand a siege, if need be.' She built the North Terrace, with a covered gallery over it, as a form of conservatory.

The Castle came into the hands of the Parliamentarians early in the Civil War by a ruse of Colonel Venn. Prince Rupert's artillery battered the town of Windsor for seven hours a few days later but his shot had no effect on the Castle. Throughout the war and the rule of major generals Windsor remained a military headquarters and a prison. Compared with the iconoclasm of Roundheads all over the country Windsor escaped very lightly. Royalist prisoners have left memorials of their confinement in the beautiful heraldic inscriptions in the chamber of the Norman Gate.

Charles II entrusted to Hugh May the task of rebuilding the royal apartments and his St. George's Hall (destroyed in 1826) and plain, box-like, Star Building, which supplanted the irregular Plantagenet quarters on the north terrace, appeared on entering to be a Little Versailles. The ceilings painted by Verrio, the carvings of Grinling Gibbons and the tapestries and pictures made the Hall so superb that it inspired Wren to take it as his model for the Painted Hall at Greenwich. One of Charles's very last acts was to order the laying out of the Long Walk, planted with elms, to provide future sovereigns with a magnificent vista (the trees, alas, had to be felled in 1945 because of a disease); a bronze equestrian statue of the King appropriately faces Charles's Star Building.

When George IV decided to move across to the Castle from Royal Lodge in 1824 his primary task was to secure privacy; as he told the Dean of Windsor, he would never have chosen to move if he was going to be overlooked and interrupted by his subjects at all hours of the day. The next task was the demolition of Queen's Lodge in the Home Park, which had been bought and used by Queen Anne as her summer retreat. George III had also lived in it before moving into the Castle proper in 1804. This enabled the Long Walk to be continued right to the Castle wall, and on his sixty-second birthday George IV laid the foundation stone of the new archway that would bring the walk right into the Quadrangle. Soon much more extensive works were planned for which Parliament voted £300,000 and Jeffry Wyatt was chosen as the architect. To distinguish himself from his uncle, James Wyatt, Jeffry asked the King's permission to change his name to Wyatville. ('Veal or mutton', replied George IV, 'Call yourself what you like.') In the next four years Windsor was transformed. The apartments on the east and south sides of the Quadrangle were rebuilt in Gothic style, which harmonizes remarkably well with the rest of the Castle, a Grand Corridor and Banqueting-rooms were added, and great changes made to the interior of Charles II's buildings on the North Terrace. He began building the George IV Gate, bringing Charles II's Long Walk right to the Quadrangle in 1824.

The Round Tower was also renovated and raised. In place of a tumble-down collection of draughty, inconvenient apartments Wyatville made a comfortable palace, and his work has stood the test of time. He had a flair for symmetry and gave the castle its characteristic distant vista. In the end the bill for these works, which included a private garden, exceeded £1,000,000.

Windsor Castle

One room was particularly magnificent. With Napoleon an exile in St. Helena, George IV had commissioned Sir Thomas Lawrence to paint a series of portraits of the allied sovereigns and commanders who had contributed to the Emperor's downfall; and one of the problems that the architects competing with designs for the new apartment were required to consider was how to create a gallery in which these portraits could be hung. The Iron Duke was himself one of the adjudicators of the plans. Wyatville, the successful competitor, decided to roof Horn Court and make it the Waterloo Chamber. Here on June 18 each year, the anniversary of the Battle, the Waterloo Dinner, attended by the most senior officers of the fighting services, is held.

Queen Victoria's long reign, most of it as 'widow of Windsor', has left two legacies: the renovated Curfew Tower, modelled on a tower at Carcasonne, which Napoleon III had been restoring when he stayed at Windsor in 1855, and secondly the Albert Memorial Chapel, to the east of St. George's, built by Sir Gilbert Scott.

Though the home of the House of Windsor, the general public is admitted to the greater part of Windsor even when the Queen is in residence, for only the private apartments overlooking the South and East Terraces are sacrosanct. Visitors can see Henry VIII's suit of armour, Queen Mary's dolls' house and exhibitions of pictures, prints and drawings. A sight of the guards parading in the quadrangle is a reminder that Windsor is still garrisoned for ceremony, if not for defence, while St. George's Chapel gives the Lower Ward the atmosphere of a cathedral close. Above all there is the Round Tower, reminding us of the origins of the castle, which down the centuries has been transformed into a comfortable palace.

Woodstock, eight miles north of Oxford, had begun as a hunting-lodge in the days when vast areas of the kingdom formed the royal forest, maintained solely for the sport of the Norman kings. The chase was not limited to deer, for boars, wolves and wildcats still prowled about England and were hunted with mixed packs of eight greyhounds and twenty-four running-hounds. The stables and kennels at Woodstock were extensive; yet a hunting-lodge had to be a building that was large enough to house the entire court for, besides the household officials, bishops, earls and a host of civil servants followed the King wherever he went to transact public business. 'Great Councils', the forerunner of Parliaments, were often held at Woodstock in the twelfth century after a hectic day's hunting.

Woodstock was the first park in England. Part of it was fenced by Henry I for his menagerie, for he was fascinated by the wonders of distant lands and begged foreign princes to present him with strange beasts. An English monk stood by the railings amazed at the lions and leopards, lynxes and camels—'creatures which England does not produce'.

Later in the twelfth century the grounds at Woodstock were embellished with a lover's bower, set in the middle of an intricate maze. Here Henry II installed the Fair Rosamund, Rosamund Clifford, a baron's daughter of great beauty, in 'a house of wonderful devising so that no man or woman might come to her but he that was

The Queen's Drawing Room at Windsor Castle. The cornice by Grinling Gibbons, the great 17th-century wood-carver, has survived, but the heavily-enriched plaster ceiling is of later date. One of the principal paintings, that of Charles I's five eldest children by Sir Anthony Van Dyck, originally hung in the King's Breakfast Chamber at Whitehall Palace.

instructed by the King, or such as were right secret with him'. Chroniclers and troubadours have woven so many tales around this fairy-tale figure that it is difficult today to separate fact from fancy. When Eleanor of Acquitaine became Queen, Rosamund lay low at Woodstock and the King went hunting rather more frequently than in his bachelor days; it was no doubt with a twinkle in his eye that Henry's justiciar defined the royal forests as 'the secret places of Kings and their great delights'. Queen Eleanor discovered her husband's adultery and according to some versions of the tale tried to poison her rival. Yet Henry was soon able to live quite openly with Rosamund, for Eleanor separated from him and kept her own court over the sea in her native Poitiers. The Fair Maid of Woodstock was buried with great pomp in the chancel of Godstow Abbey church. According to tradition King Henry himself composed the neat couplet that was engraved on her splendid tombstone; it was a typical medieval pun on her name:

> This tomb doth here enclose
> The world's most beauteous rose;
> Rose passing sweet erewhile,
> Now naught but odour vile.

Progressing as they did from one palace to another no king or queen was ever at Woodstock for more than a few days at a time. The longest continuous residence of anyone was the forced stay of Princess Elizabeth, the future Queen, during her sister's reign. She had been suspected of complicity in Wyatt's Rebellion and Mary, thinking that so popular a figure would be a constant source of trouble if confined in London, had her moved from the Tower to Oxfordshire in May 1554. She remained at Woodstock, a close prisoner, for eleven months, under a strict custodian, Sir Henry Bedingfield.

To the annoyance of his Secretary of State, Sir Robert Cecil, James I was frequently at Woodstock for the hunting. Cecil thought the house far too dilapidated and poky for royalty. 'The place is unwholesome', he wrote on his first stay there with the King, '—all the house standing upon springs. It is unsavoury, for there is no savour but the cows and pigs. It is uneaseful, for only the King and Queen, with the Privy Chamber ladies and some three or four of the Scotch Council are lodged in the house, and neither chamberlain nor one English councillor have a room.' Sir Robert hated roughing it. He had fixed ideas of what a palace should be like and in a year or two sold his own country house at Theobalds, also in good hunting country, to the King. James settled Woodstock on his eldest son, Prince Henry, who celebrated the event with a series of entertainments. For several days running he feasted courtiers in a large summer-house made of green boughs—reminiscent of Rosamund's Bower.

In its last days as a palace Woodstock suffered considerable damage during a siege in the Civil War. And when in 1649 the Parliamentary surveyors arrived to take stock of the buildings the house was barely inhabitable. For want of the usual domestic quarters they turned the King's Bedroom into a kitchen and the Privy Council Room into a brewhouse.

Right in the heart of Royalist country Cromwell's officials found the tenants bemoaning the fate of their old master and bent on making life troublesome for 'the

For five centuries Woodstock manor was visited by the sovereign. Henry II (left) installed his Fair Rosamund in a lover's bower built in the grounds, and, less romantically, the young Elizabeth was held prisoner there. These drawings (right and below) show it almost totally demolished, as it was before 1714, when it was finally destroyed on the instruction of Sarah, Duchess of Marlborough, during the building of Blenheim Palace in the Park.

usurpers'. There was in the park a massive tree which generations of Woodstock boys and girls had learnt from their fathers to call the King's Oak; and on the day King Charles was executed a wreath of evergreens was placed at the foot of the trunk. The Roundhead surveyors promptly had the tree uprooted, 'that nothing might remain that had the name of King attached to it'. But the night after the oak was felled the surveyors' beds moved uncannily, the sheets were soaked with stagnant pond water and the curtains were pulled to and fro all night.

The new owners pulled down most of the buildings for the sake of the stone, leaving only the gatehouse in which Queen Elizabeth had been imprisoned and a few adjoining rooms. At the Restoration Lord Lovelace made an attractive house out of this surviving fragment of the old palace.

The *coup de grace* was given by Sarah, Duchess of Marlborough. For his victory at Blenheim rewards were heaped on the Duke and by a special Act of Parliament the ancient manor of Woodstock was transferred to him. Queen Anne went one better than her ministers and instructed Sir John Vanbrugh to build a palace for Marlborough in Woodstock Park at her own expense. When Blenheim Palace was being built the architect spent some £2,000 on repairs to what remained of the old palace of Woodstock. But one day the Treasurer, Godolphin, while staying at the still unfinished Blenheim, remarked to Duchess Sarah that it was a pity the view was spoilt by a pile of ruins. She agreed with him and ordered the old gatehouse to be demolished. Not a stone remains to remind the modern visitor to Blenheim that he is walking over the spot where Henry II and Rosamund made love, where Elizabeth the Prisoner pined for an English Bible and King James made himself ill through eating too much fruit.

Caernarvon Castle

The Principality is rich in castles, but only that at Caernarvon, 'the boast of North Wales', near the south-west of the Menai Strait, can properly be reckoned among former royal houses. When Edward I was subduing the country after defeating the Welsh princes in 1283, Caernarvon was a natural site for a castle, for the Romans had once founded a military station in this area and a thousand years later Hugh, Earl of Chester had built a considerable fort here during the short-lived Norman conquest of Wales. Edward began building eight castles as bastions for holding the country against the chieftains who had fought for Llewelyn—Flint and Rhuddlan, Aberystwyth and Builth, Conway, Harlech and Beaumaris—but Caernarvon was rather different from these. It was intended to be as much a palace as a fortress and was regarded as the centre for the future administration of North Wales.

The original architect was James of St. George, a military engineer from Savoy, who copied for Edward I some of the features of the 'Crusader Castles' which the King had seen in the Holy Land. Instead of the traditional Anglo-Norman system of concentric defence, he devised a single defensive area, divided into two wards by a cross wall. Much of the limestone came by boat from Anglesey and there was a ready supply of local puddingstone. The work was continued under Walter of Hereford's direction, being completed in 1327 at a total cost of £19,000. Though neither great hall nor chapel survive, the massive walls with seven angular towers remain an imposing sight. Dr. Johnson who saw the ruins two centuries ago, before maintenance was begun, called Caernarvon 'an edifice of stupendous majesty and strength'.

The King's Gate was defended by a drawbridge over the moat with six portcullises, and the Eagle Tower, named from a sculpture on its walls, is a remarkable citadel in itself, standing 128 feet high. Because the Eagle Tower forms the finest part of the remains, tradition assigns to it the distinction of being the birthplace of Edward of Caernarvon, the future Edward II, on St. Mark's Day 1284. He was certainly born within the precincts of the castle, whither his warrior father had summoned Queen Eleanor, but at the time of her lying-in the Eagle Tower was far from completion. Legend again credits Edward I with the intention of making political capital of the birth, but at the time Edward of Caernarvon was not heir to the throne. Sixteen years later he created him Prince of Wales on February 7, 1301, and ordered him to return to the Principality to receive the homage of his tenants. The next effective Prince of Wales, Arthur Tudor, elder brother of the future Henry VIII, ruled Wales not from Caernarvon but from Ludlow.

At Caernarvon Castle in 1637 William Prynne, the Puritan, was imprisoned for seditious writings which had also cost him his ears; it was to have been a life sentence, but the demonstrations in his favour at Caernarvon so alarmed the government that Prynne was removed to Jersey. The Castle changed hands several times during the Civil War and on his restoration Charles II ordered the demolition of the buildings. This order was disregarded, on grounds of expense, so the Castle has remained to become the pride of the Royal Commission on Ancient Monuments for Wales.

Six hundred and ten years after Edward of Caernarvon's presentation to the Welsh people the future Edward VIII was invested as Prince of Wales at the Castle, a ceremony repeated for Prince Charles in 1969.

Caernarvon Castle is magnificently sited on a commanding promontory where the river Seiont flows into the Menai Straits. The illustration (right) shows it as it was in 1774, engraved by R. Godfrey, and (below) as it is today, largely unaltered but for the clearance of ancient houses built against its walls.

Caernarvon Castle

In past centuries an extensive area of the Strand, running north and west from what is now Waterloo Bridge, formed the Liberty of the Savoy, a veritable buffer-state between the cities of London and Westminster. Today the sole reminders of the former glories of the Liberty are the Savoy Chapel and the modern Duchy of Lancaster Building. A house had been built here in 1246 by Peter, Count of Savoy, who was uncle to Queen Eleanor of Provence, the wife of Henry III. The count had bequeathed this valuable property to the hospice of Great St. Bernard at Montjoux in his native Savoy, but Eleanor redeemed this gift for 200 marks in 1270 and later assigned 'the place called the Sauvoye' to her son Edmund, the first Earl of Lancaster, who both extended and fortified it.

In the middle years of the fourteenth century his successor, Henry Plantagenet, first Duke of Lancaster, spent the lavish sum of £35,000 in the currency of the day on improvements—about £2 million in today's terms—from booty acquired during campaigning in France. With its great hall, chapel and cloister, its fine gardens and fishpond, the Savoy was reckoned the finest residence in the Kingdom. Beyond the hall were the private apartments, looking out over pleasant terraces to the distant river, with the Palace's own water stairs and landing place. On Henry's death the Palace passed to his daughter Blanche who had married Edward III's warrior son, John of Gaunt. King John of France, captured after the battle of Poitiers, died here

The Eagle Tower of Caernarvon Castle was built in the late 13th century, while the photograph shows it as it appeared six centuries later.

The Savoy has been in royal possession for centuries, the land first being granted to Peter of Savoy, uncle of Henry III's queen, Eleanor of Provence, in 1246. Henry, the first Duke of Lancaster, built a fine palace on the site but it was plundered and burnt down during Wat Tyler's rebellion in 1381. A hospital was built here by Henry VII in the early 16th century, and at the time this drawing was made in 1650 it was still so used. The chapel alone, of which only part is the original, now remains.

as a prisoner. The fate of the Savoy was sealed during the Peasants' Revolt when Wat Tyler's men out of hatred of Gaunt set the Palace on fire, though certain buildings, including Simeon's Tower and the gaol escaped destruction.

The rebuilding of the site was shirked for a century and a quarter until Henry VII endowed the Savoy as an almshouse for 100 paupers and built the chapel, of which only the shell remains. Henry's foundation survived the upheaval of the Reformation but was finally suppressed in 1702. By then it had become a refuge for debtors and 'a chief nursery' of evil-doers. Before then room had been found within its walls for such different establishments as the Marshalsea Prison, the office of the King's printer, a German Lutheran church, a place of worship for the Persian ambassador—probably a mosque—a Jesuit school, for no more than thirty months, and soldiers' quarters. The dormitory of the former hospital continued to be used as a barracks until much later. In the mid-eighteenth century the chapel became celebrated as the easiest place in the Kingdom in which to be married—a veritable Gretna Green—so that in 1755 no fewer than 1,190 couples were married there. The buildings, with the exception of the chapel, were pulled down when old Waterloo Bridge was built in 1815. The chapel itself has been extensively restored over the last two centuries, especially after a serious fire in 1864, and one of the windows commemorates the connexion with the neighbourhood of those two Savoyards, Gilbert and Sullivan.

Eltham Palace

The old palace at Eltham in Kent had belonged to the bishops of Durham in the earlier middle ages and proved a pleasant retreat for successive prince bishops who braved the long journey to the capital for Parliament and Council. Anthony Bek, bishop at the turn of the thirteenth century, had improved Eltham beyond all recognition, but in 1305 he decided to make a present of the buildings to Edward of Caernarvon, the future Edward II, to safeguard his already great preferments in church and state.

With its moated inner court, its great hall and its spacious apartments Eltham became the most magnificent of the King's country houses. Twice in the fourteenth century it was the meeting-place of Parliament, and here 2,000 courtiers would sometimes share the royal table at Christmas. In the park which down the years provided so many seasoned oaks for the navy, successive kings indulged in their favourite sport—stag-hunting. In the grounds tournaments were held and distinguished visitors entertained. It is hard for the modern visitor to think that a Byzantine Emperor once gaped at the splendour of the buildings.

Henry VII was often here with his family for he had spent what for him were considerable sums on renovations, but his son thought the buildings, with the exception of the hall, with its fine hammer-beam roof, very cramped. Soon after his accession he demolished the old chapel, replacing it with one having 'comely windows, most chapel-like, as well at the high altar as on both sides'. One day Henry ordered the workmen 'to take away the hill' on the south side of the orchard, as it spoilt the view. Tunnels were dug to take the refuse from the kitchen beneath the moat. By the end of these operations Eltham was the most comfortable and up to date of the King's homes. Here in 1525 he approved the Eltham Ordinances, largely devised by Cardinal

The restored Great Hall of Eltham Palace, showing its magnificent 15th-century hammer-beam roof.

Wolsey, which effected a root and branch reform in the running of the royal household.

As Greenwich grew in royal favour, neighbouring Eltham lost its importance. Soon King Henry visited Eltham merely to hunt in the park, and after the day's sport went back to Greenwich to sleep. Queen Elizabeth rarely slept there and the Palace subsequently fell into decay. When it was confiscated by Parliament after Charles I's execution, the royal apartments were barren of furniture, most of the fabric was beyond repair, the gardens were a wilderness and the moat stagnant. The Palace was sold for its stone, tiles and other materials. Before long the tenant who farmed the lands chose to live in the new red-brick Lodge built by Hugh May in 1663–4, and the great hall became used as a barn. Not until the 1930s was a systematic programme of renovations put in hand. The Palace where Henry Tudor had entertained Erasmus has now become the headquarters of the Institute of Army Education.

Sheen & Richmond

Kew Palace in Surrey (*see p. 106*) is the sole survivor of a series of royal homes on this riverside site. It is not even the last of the series, for at the beginning of the nineteenth century George III embarked on a massive castellated palace to the south, which was demolished before it had been completed. Centuries earlier the entire estate had formed part of the royal manor of Sheen, a name deriving from the Anglo-Saxon word for a beauty spot, which in time was supplanted by Henry Tudor's Palace of Richmond.

Sheen Palace was a favourite home of both Edward III, who died there, and of Richard II until the tragic death of his consort, Anne of Bohemia. In a frenzy of grief Richard ordered the buildings to be pulled down to show the world how great was his personal loss. He never discovered that his orders had not been effectively carried out; the dead Queen's apartments were certainly razed to the ground, but other quarters were spared. It was left to Henry V to have the rubble cleared away to make way for 'a curious and costly building'. North of the palace Henry endowed a Carthusian monastery, the House of Jesus of Bethlehem of Sheen, and opposite, on the Middlesex bank of the river, he established a nunnery, Sion House.

Henry VII had planned to keep Christmas at Sheen in 1498, but on the night of December 21, while the royal family was in residence, fire broke out. The place was gutted and much valuable furniture was lost, though no one was killed. The King decided to replace the ruined manor-house by a magnificent residence in the Gothic style, to be built, like a college, round a paved court. Within two years the new palace was ready for occupation. Henry has a reputation for carefulness in money matters, but here nothing was skimped; there was lead in plenty on the roof, and the number of windows would have made contemporaries regard the building as a crystal palace. The royal quarters, the Privy Lodging, were decorated with fourteen turrets; and the chapel, unlike any parish church of the time, had pews ('handsome cathedral seats'). Here Henry kept his library, with its great collection of French works. But the chief feature of the Palace was the Tower; and those privileged to climb the 120 steps enjoyed a wonderful view.

To crown his achievement Henry VII, in the manner of a dictator, changed the name. At the time of Bosworth he had been Earl of Richmond, the Yorkshire honour, but with his accession this title had merged in the Crown. He now perpetuated the name by decreeing that what had previously been termed Sheen should from henceforth be known as Richmond Palace.

In her later years Elizabeth I found that her grandfather's palace suited her health better than anywhere else, perhaps because her astrologer, Dr. Dee, commended it so warmly. When January snows made Whitehall cheerless and even Greenwich bleak she removed herself to Richmond—that 'warm winter box to shelter her old age'. Her godson, James I, assigned Richmond to Prince Henry, then his heir, while on the other side of the park, at Kew, his sister Elizabeth, soon to be 'Winter Queen' of Bohemia, had her own establishment. A generation later the future Charles II was at Richmond studying the Bible with Bishop Duppa.

Under Cromwell people began filching stone from the site so that it was far too dilapidated for Henrietta Maria to live in when she returned to England. Spending

Richmond Palace. After the fire of 1497, which totally destroyed the old building, Henry VII ordered it to be rebuilt on a magnificent scale. A contemporary described it as 'this ertheley and secunde Paradise', adding that it was 'most glorious and joyefull to consider and beholde'.

A doorway with Jacobean surrounds, and (far right) part of the Wardrobe of Richmond Palace, which was restored in the 18th century.

36

RICHMOND

vast sums on her dower houses at Greenwich and Somerset House she had nothing left for repairing Richmond; it crumbled away and soon only the lodge was standing. This was leased to Lady Villiers, governess of the future Queen Anne; when she became heir to the throne at the Revolution Anne tried in vain to secure the lodge for herself as 'she loved it in her infancy and the air agreed with her'. But the glories of Richmond had passed and boys played cricket on the spot where knights at arms had held a tournament.

The Gatehouse of Richmond Palace. Here in the room above the Gateway, according to local legend, died Queen Elizabeth, who made the Palace one of her principal homes and who referred to it as her 'warm winter-box'.

2   *The House of Tudor*

By the end of the Middle Ages there were no more than six royal residences in regular use, but the new monarchy of the Tudors completely altered the situation so that by the death of Henry VIII the crown had acquired seven additional homes, two of them in the fast-growing capital. Though renowned for his cautious spending, Henry VII had found money to renovate Humphrey, Duke of Gloucester's house, Placentia, which he renamed Greenwich, and rebuilt Richmond, as we have seen. His son, deprived of essential accommodation by the great fire at Westminster in 1512, browbeat Cardinal Wolsey into parting with York House, which he renamed Whitehall, and Hampton Court. St. James's Palace was a windfall of the Dissolution of the Monasteries. Besides the manor houses of Oatlands in Surrey and of Hunsdon and Hatfield in Hertfordshire, which Henry bought as safe retreats for his family from the plague of London, he built Nonsuch, an extravagant Renaissance masterpiece, stamped with his personality. Henry VIII's costly building programme was only made possible by the increased revenue that the Dissolution brought. Such was a goodly heritage for his children who made no attempt to extend it and before long there were complaints that the ordinary revenues of the crown were insufficient for the upkeep of the palaces.

Greenwich

Many royal homes have a military background, but Greenwich is the only one with naval connexions, and so it is fitting that the white ensign should fly from the flag-staff of the riverside palace in its old days. Henry V acquired the lands lying in this great loop of the Thames in 1414, when he confiscated the endowments of the alien priories, and granted most of the Greenwich estate to his youngest brother, Humphrey, Duke of Gloucester, who gradually built Bella Court, an imposing residence with embattled walls, fit for the Regent of the infant Henry VI. Duke Humphrey left his rich collection of books to Oxford University, but Bella Court passed to his enemy, Queen Margaret of Anjou.

Margaret made far-reaching improvements. There was now glass in the windows—the height of luxury—and the floors were all covered with terra-cotta tiles bearing her monogram. The exterior was ornamented with pillars sculptured with her heraldic flower, the marguerite. To the west she built a pier giving access to the river at all states of the tide. Significantly, on becoming royal property, the name of the Palace was changed; Bella Court became Placentia (or Pleasance). The residents of Placentia changed with the fortunes of the Wars of the Roses until in 1485 Henry Tudor moved in and changed the name to Greenwich Palace. Early in his reign he refaced the entire building with red brick; his son added a tilt-yard and an armoury.

Queen Elizabeth I, who had been born at Greenwich in 1533, remained very attached to the house and held many functions of the royal year here. Her successor settled the palace on his Queen, in 1613, to mark their belated reconciliation. Since James VI was about to spend freely on improvements to his house at Newmarket, Queen Anne of Denmark persuaded him it was only fair that she should have money for major alterations at Greenwich, which had remained unchanged for a century.

Hitherto Greenwich had seemed to be all frontage and no depth, but the Palace gardens to the south were now to be linked with the park by an imposing house.

The Old Palace at Greenwich. It was first known as 'Bella Court' and later as 'Placentia'. Henry VIII was born here and so were his daughters, Princess Mary and Elizabeth. During the Interregnum it suffered badly and was pulled down on direction of Charles II.

(Above, right). *In the painting by an unknown artist of the time of James I the Old Palace at Greenwich can be seen as a jumble of buildings by the river. On the hill can be seen a hunting lodge known as Duke Humphrey's Tower which was later pulled down to make way for Wren's Observatory.*

Two sketches by John Webb, Inigo Jones' pupil, for the Palace of Greenwich.

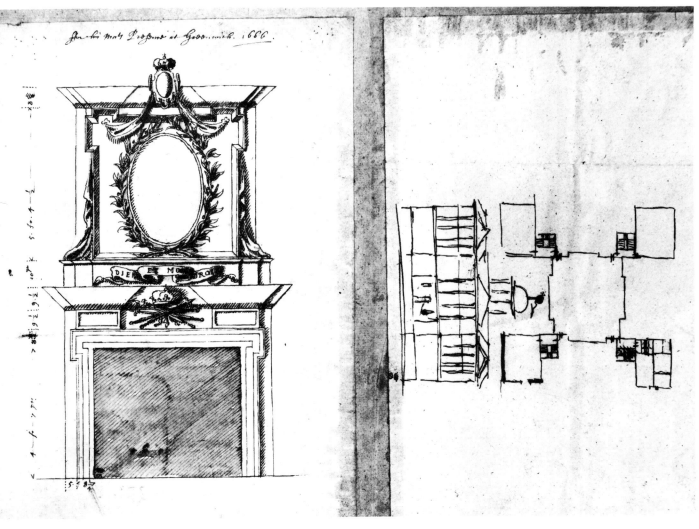

Greenwich

(Above). *Greenwich Palace painted by Henry Danckerts in 1670. The house in the foreground is the Queen's House, through which passes a road dividing the Park from the Palace garden. Beyond is the uncompleted King Charles building (1663).*

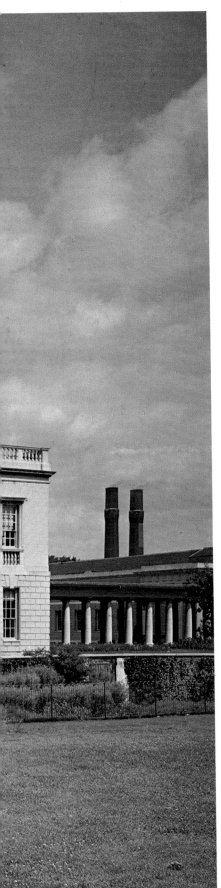

(Left). *Queen's House, Greenwich— 'The House of Delight' built for James I's consort, Queen Anne of Denmark, though not completed in her lifetime. The designer of this sublime building was Inigo Jones (1573–1652), who worked on a number of royal commissions and was the first to introduce the new vogue for classical design to England.*

'She is building somewhat at Greenwich', wrote a courtier, 'which must be finished this summer, that is to be some curious device of Inigo Jones and will cost above £4,000.' Between the gardens and the park ran the Deptford-Woolwich road by which there stood an old gatehouse. The architect swept this aside to make way for the House of Delight (or Queen's House), one of the finest examples of Renaissance architecture in England; today it contains the National Maritime Museum.

Anne of Denmark died in 1618 before her House of Delight was ready for occupation. The task of completion was laid aside for ten years. Meanwhile Charles I had settled Greenwich on his wife (once again his was a symbolic present after differences between husband and wife had been made up), and Inigo Jones returned to his scheme. The building was in fact *two* houses, joined by a covered bridge, for the road passed beneath the thirty-foot connecting archway. The Queen could thus pass into the park at the south or into the Palace gardens at the north, as if this highway had never existed. An Italian loggia, designed (in the architect's words) as 'a frontispiece in the midst', gave a splendid view across the park. In 1661 two further bridges were to be built over the road, and today, with the road diverted, it is difficult to realize that the Queen's House was originally two separate buildings. Inigo Jones had taken the greatest care over the interior and himself designed the beautiful chimney-pieces and supervised the elaborate carvings, and the ceilings of the entrance hall and the Queen's closet were painted by Gentileschi. The black and white marble paving on the floors of the entrance hall put every other English palace to shame. The pictures on the wall included a Rubens. It was certainly a House of Delight, yet ironically Henrietta had barely time to enjoy it before she had to flee to France with the coming of the Civil War.

The Queen's House became the home of Bulstrode Whitelocke, a leading councillor of Cromwell's; parts of the older palace by the river were parcelled out to lesser fry, while the rest was used for Dutch prisoners of war.

At the Restoration the derelict palace by the river was demolished and orders were given for the enlargement of the Queen's House. This task was entrusted to John Webb, son-in-law and pupil of Inigo Jones, who had inherited the master's drawings. Attic rooms were built and some of the larger state rooms were partitioned. The most remarkable feature was to be the addition of pavilions at the corners, but this project was later abandoned. The house remained the property of the Queen Mother; a few years later, however, Webb began building a new block for King Charles. Shortage of money once more delayed the completion of the new Greenwich, though a part of the Palace was sufficiently ready to house the Admiralty during the Plague. In subsequent years Pepys often revisited Greenwich on his way to and from the dock-yards and commented that 'the King's House goes on slow, but is very pretty'.

The gardens were, however, successfully relaid in the French style with the help of Le Nôtre, the denuded park replanted and a 'snow well' built there; this was probably the first refrigerator in England. On a hill in the park the King established his observatory. Here Sir John Flamsteed, the first of a distinguished line of astronomers royal, began making observations. But Charles II's interest in Greenwich waned and nothing was spent on the works for the last ten years of the reign.

William and Mary inherited the legacy of the unfinished works at Greenwich and with the rebuilding of Hampton Court and a new palace at Kensington they could ill afford to carry out Charles's grand design. By a happy decision Mary found a new use for the site. As a thank-offering to the Royal Navy for saving the throne by its services at Barfleur and La Hogue she presented all the riverside area, including the Charles II block, to the senior service for an infirmary for wounded seamen. Thus from the rubble of Duke Humphrey's Bella Court arose Greenwich Hospital.

The Hospital buildings were Wren's greatest triumph, and most glorious of all was the painted hall with its ceiling decorated by Sir James Thornhill. The painting took so long to complete at £3 per yard—the total cost was £6,085—that it included the scene of George I's landing at Greenwich as well as portraits of William and Mary. Here the disabled of the naval wars of the eighteenth century found a refuge.

In 1805 Caroline, Princess of Wales, sold the Queen's House to the Royal Naval Asylum (then in Paddington) for £7,875 so that it might be adapted as a school for seamen's children. The Asylum later became amalgamated with the Greenwich Hospital School and remained here until 1933 when Inigo Jones's building became the National Maritime Museum. At once the Trustees began to rediscover the glorious features of the old house, such as the painted ceiling in the Queen's bedroom. The modern visitor can enjoy the splendours of Henrietta Maria's house, much as it was in the seventeenth century, and at the same time see a great collection of pictures, documents, models and apparatus which illustrate Britain's naval heritage.

York Place had been the London residence of the Archbishop of York for three centuries, but it was only under the last Pre-Reformation Archbishop, Thomas Wolsey, that it came to outshine every other home in the capital. His sovereign had watched the building of a massive great hall and the lavish improvements to the site with envious eyes in the years after the fire at Westminster Palace, and then, dissatisfied at the progress of the negotiations with the Pope for his divorce from Catherine of Aragon, Henry at last decided to dismiss the Cardinal from his high office and banish him from court. In November 1529 King Henry moved into York Place.

At once Henry embarked on an ambitious programme of rebuilding: 'the plan is on so large a scale', wrote one onlooker, 'that many thousands of houses will be levelled'; covering twenty-four acres, it was the biggest palace in Christendom. The Supreme Head of the Church could improve on what a cardinal had accomplished. During the rebuilding of the Treasury in 1962, the original Tudor tennis court and wine cellars were at last laid bare. A new embankment was made on the riverside, with two landing-places for the royal barge. A turretted gateway now commanded the entrance from the street, though the King could not interfere with the public right-of-way from Whitehall Stairs on the river through the Palace grounds to the street gate. Land was acquired on the west side of the street, overlooking St. James's Park; and this new property which housed the tilt-yard and the tennis courts, a cock-pit and a bowling alley, was connected with the Palace by two gateways across Whitehall—The King Street and the Holbein Gate. (It is now clear that the artist did not design the latter, but probably had rooms in it while he was painting ceilings in the royal apartments). An Italian who visited the Palace in 1531 was thrilled by the splendours to be seen on every side. He marvelled at 'three so-called porticos, and halls without chambers, the windows on each side looking on to gardens and the river; the ceiling marvellously wrought in stone with gold, and the wainscot of carved wood representing a thousand beautiful figures, and round about these are chambers and very large halls, all hung with tapestries'.

All signs of Wolsey's occupation were swept away and within the year even the name of York Place had been changed. In those years of the Reformation when the modern state was emerging Whitehall Palace symbolized the power of the new monarchy. Under the Tudors, as today, the name 'Whitehall' was synonymous with government.

Until the early seventeenth century there was no permanent banqueting hall, and for special occasions temporary structures of canvas and timber were erected in the grounds. The first stone banqueting hall built by James I had a short life. In January 1619 two workmen were ordered to clear up the debris after the usual series of Christmas masques. To save themselves trouble they had a bonfire of the rubbish inside the building, and at once realized their foolishness—the place was in flames and they shut the doors and ran to hide. The Lord Chamberlain took command of the scene and prevented the fire from spreading to neighbouring buildings, but it was impossible to save the Banqueting-House. The new building, designed by Inigo Jones, was completed in three years at a cost of £15,000. The only part of the Palace to

Inigo Jones' masterpiece, the Banqueting-House, Whitehall, was opened in 1622. Though entirely refaced in unsympathetic Portland stone in the 19th century, the details of the original are faithfully preserved. The interior (left) has also been restored to its original appearance after numerous alterations, and superbly displays the painted ceiling by Sir Peter Paul Rubens, which was completed in 1634 and commemorates allegorically the virtues of James I.

survive it, was until recently the Museum of the Royal United Service Institution, but is now in use again for government receptions. It is one of the half dozen master-pieces of English architecture; as the exterior had worn badly it was refaced by Sir John Soane in 1829 with Portland stone, a deft matching of the original work so that few appreciate that the façade is not exactly as Inigo Jones had left it. On the ceiling Rubens painted nine panels representing the peace and prosperity of James's reign.

Inigo Jones was later to build the Clock House, a gallery with a timbered staircase leading to St. James's Park and a playhouse, converted from the Tudor cockpit. With the Civil War, Whitehall was deserted. 'A Palace without a Presence', said a pamphleteer in 1642, 'You may walk into the Presence Chamber with your hat, spurs and sword on. And if you will presume to be so unmannerly, you may sit down in the Chair of State.' By 1648 troops were being quartered there and before the year was out King Charles was a prisoner in his own palace, awaiting his trial. His execution on January 30, 1649, is the most remarkable event in the whole history of Whitehall. Oliver Cromwell at first had rooms in the Cockpit but as Lord Protector he lived in regal state in Whitehall.

Whitehall

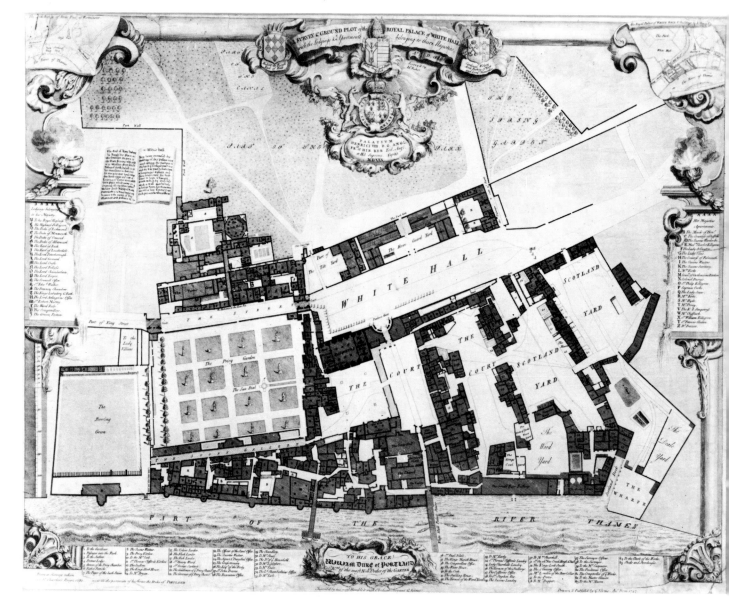

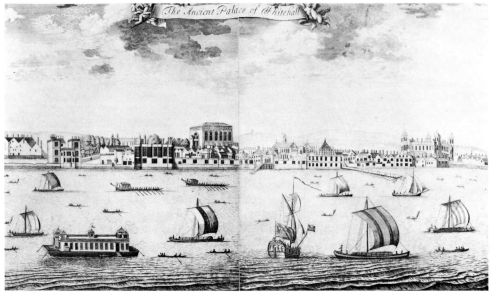

A singularly inaccurate drawing of Whitehall at the beginning of the 18th century.

(Left). A plan of the Royal Palace of Whitehall before the disastrous fire of 1698 which destroyed all the ancient timber houses, and, of the principal buildings, only left the Banqueting-House and the Holbein and Whitehall Gates intact.

(Right). The Banqueting-House which was used as the main ceremonial centre of Government in the 17th century.

The Palace came into its own at the Restoration. Charles II, who made it his principal residence, lavished money on interior decorations. Both Evelyn and Pepys recorded in detail the splendid setting for the most luxurious and extravagant court that England has ever seen. Given the money Charles intended rebuilding the entire Palace; and if Whitehall, as he was forced to leave it, lacked the magnificence of Versailles, it still covered an area more than three times the size of the French palace. Eventually the most splendid apartments of all were those at the end of the Matted Gallery belonging to the Breton beauty, Louise de Kéroualle, later Duchess of Portsmouth. Three times in her reign she had them rebuilt to satisfy her wildly extravagant tastes. Here among the costly Gobelin tapestries, the pictures which Queen Catherine had unwillingly lent her, the oriental furniture and a profusion of gold and silver knick-knacks on her dressing-table, Louise kept her court.

Charles was content to adapt his own quarters to his tastes, enjoying the privacy of his Closet, where he kept his collection of clocks and instruments, and the time spent in his private laboratory. By the end of the reign he had postponed indefinitely the idea of rebuilding here, for he had set Wren to work at Winchester. James II recalled Wren to Whitehall to undertake a new block, facing the Privy Garden (with its curious sun dial), running from the Holbein Gate to the river. Some £35,000 was spent on this development, which included a chapel enriched with carvings by Grinling Gibbons. Wren also built a small court behind the Banqueting-House, with a council chamber.

These new buildings, and many of the old, perished in the fire of January 4–5, 1698. Fire engines pumping Thames water could not check the flames which swept right from the Privy Stairs to the corner of the Banqueting-House, from the Privy Gardens to Scotland Yard. Casualties were mercifully few—not more than thirty persons, including the Dutchwoman, who had caused the fire, perished. Soldiers saved hundreds of people from certain death by preventing them from entering buildings to rescue property. For seventeen hours the buildings blazed. To try and confine the flames certain houses were blown up with gunpowder. All that remained was the Banqueting-House—though even that was damaged—and the Whitehall and Holbein Gates. Very few of the pictures, curios and the priceless bric-à-brac with which successive sovereigns had filled the state apartments were saved. 'Whitehall burnt: nothing but walls and ruins left', wrote Evelyn almost in tears—the tersest entry in his whole *Diary*. Looters picked over the charred remains and one of them stumbled on a gold bust of Wolsey.

King William III visiting the ruins swore that with God's help a new Whitehall would rise like a phoenix from the ashes; yet in a letter to a friend he recalled that the accident 'affected him less than it might another, because Whitehall was a place in which he could not live'. Sir Christopher Wren, who had risked his life trying to save the old palace, and Hawksmoor were ordered to prepare plans for a new, and contrived 'a sweeping unity of design' in their drawings. Had Mary II still been alive there is little doubt that rebuilding would have begun but William, as a Dutchman, could never appreciate the historical significance of Whitehall and the plans were shelved.

'It is a dismal sight', wrote a Londoner, 'to behold such a glorious, famous, and most renowned Palace reduced to a heap of rubbish and ashes, which the day before might justly contend with any palace in the world for riches, honour, nobility and grandeur'. It was years before the ruins were cleared, and while the going was good Vanbrugh petitioned for a vacant lot and built his Goose-Pie House. But if the site was no longer the home of the sovereign, it remained the home of government. Already before the fire the first Admiralty had been erected and very gradually during the next two centuries one government department after another became quartered in the old Palace grounds. Where Henry VIII had played tennis and Charles II had watched Nell Gwynn act from his royal box stands William Kent's Treasury, built in 1734 and thoroughly renovated a few years ago; where James I had watched bear-baiting arose the Horse Guards in 1751. A vast modern block, on the other side of the street covers three courts of the Stuart palace.

The removal of the King's Street and Holbein Gates (in 1723 and 1759) allowed Whitehall to develop in time as a busy thoroughfare, except for Remembrance Sunday each November when the Queen, following the tradition set by her grand-father in 1921, lays a wreath of Flanders poppies by Sir Edwin Lutyens' Cenotaph.

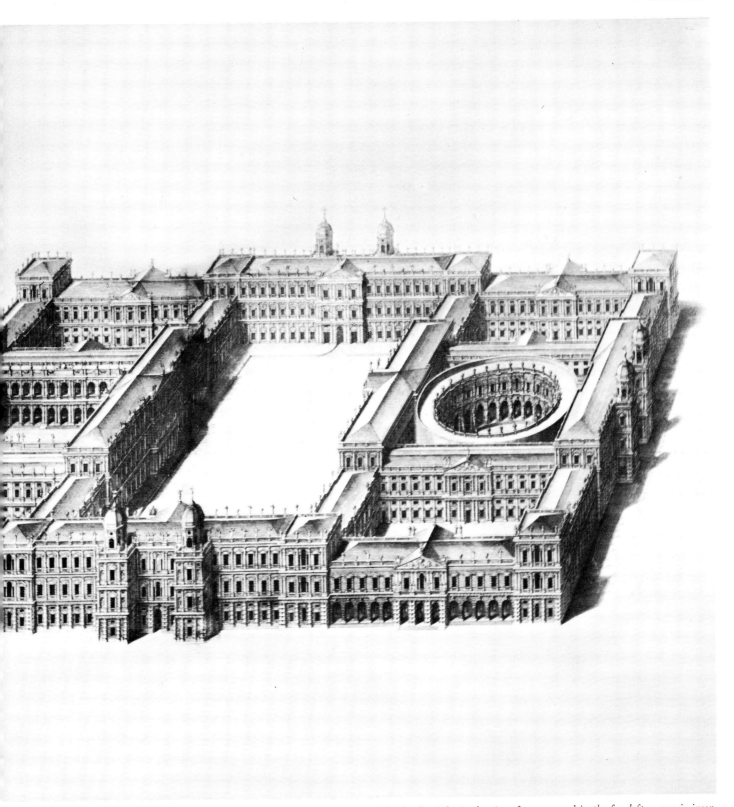

A view of Inigo Jones' design of 1638 for a massive royal palace at Whitehall. To the right is the river frontage, and in the far left corner is incorporated the Banqueting-House. However, Charles I never had the resources to construct such a grand concept.

Hampton Court

Hampton Court was another spoil from Wolsey's fall. The red-brick manor-house, set in a spacious park by the river opposite the town of Kingston, was even more magnificent than York Place. The state rooms were 'all hung with tapestry which is changed once a week' and there were costly Damascene carpets on the floor. Even the water brought by a private pipeline was far fresher than that supplied to any of the King's residences. The building and its furnishings had cost the Cardinal 200,000 gold crowns. As a desperate attempt to retain Henry's favour, Wolsey offered Hampton to him with its entire contents. This gift, the most handsome that a subject has ever made to a monarch, was greedily accepted, and once in his possession the King gave instructions for its extension and complete redecoration. All over the Palace workmen were busy erasing the Cardinal's personal emblems and setting up the royal arms and the King's beasts. Henry not only moved into the Cardinal's town and country houses but also took over the absolute power which in his heyday Wolsey had wielded in Church and State. The rebuilt Palace at Hampton, like the new Whitehall, symbolized Tudor despotism.

Henry VIII's Hampton was almost as extensive as the modern palace. At prodigious cost state apartments went steadily forward. Henry himself took over the first floor, Queen Katherine was assigned the second and Princess Mary the ground floor which, unlike the ground floor at Westminster was never flooded by river water. The Great Hall that replaced Wolsey's hall took five years to build, and to complete it in the time, shifts of masons and carpenters worked by candlelight. This Hall, with its elaborately carved roof and musicians' gallery, was Henry's *tour de force*. The Cardinal's kitchen was deemed to be insufficient for catering for the royal household—even though it was 48 feet long—and a second kitchen was added. The Supreme Head of the Church had the Chapel embellished with a wonderful fan-vaulted wooden ceiling. Thomas Cromwell was appalled at the cost of all these works to his royal master. 'What a great charge it is to the king', he wrote, 'to continue his buildings in so many places at once. How proud and false the workmen be; and if the King would spare for one year how profitable it would be to him.'

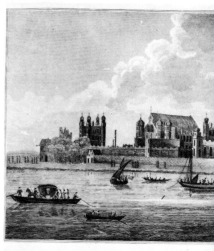

A closed tennis court was constructed with twelve windows to let in the light, protected by wire netting. There were also an open-air tennis court and three bowling-alleys, while to the north of the Palace was the tilt-yard where tournaments and joustings were held.

A recurrent theme in the history of the Palace is that of the royal honeymoon, for Mary brought Philip of Spain here after their marriage at Winchester, Charles I carried the fifteen-year-old Henrietta Maria over the threshold of Hampton in 1625 and his son arrived there on his thirty-second birthday with his Portuguese bride. The really outstanding event was the conference of divines, called together by James I in 1604, which showed that Episcopacy and Puritanism were uneasy bedfellows, yet had as its legacy the Authorized Version of the Bible.

Hampton Court came into its own with the Glorious Revolution of 1688, when William and Mary were jointly proclaimed King and Queen. William III, deeming it a healthy spot, decided he and Mary would live here provided the place were modernized. Mary was the moving spirit behind entrusting the work to Sir

(Top, above). '*A view of Hampton Court as finished by King Henry VIIIth*', drawn by Hollar, who was such an excellent draughtsman we can take this as being an accurate representation of the Palace.

(Above). The old palace of Hampton Court by the Thames in the 17th century, before the major reconstruction undertaken by Sir Christopher Wren. It was here that Charles I brought his fifteen-year-old French bride, Henrietta Maria, for their honeymoon in 1625, and from here in 1647 the King eluded his captors, Cromwell's Roundheads, and escaped across the river by boat.

(Right). *Anne Boleyn's Gateway. Before this unfortunate Queen's lodgings were complete she had been divorced and beheaded. The Gateway contains the famous astronomical clock made for Henry VIII in 1540 by Nicholas Oursian. It was designed to tell the hour, date and month, the number of days since the beginning of the year, phases of the moon and the time of high water at London Bridge.*

Hampton Court

Christopher Wren who drew up far-reaching plans on the model of the Louvre, and in June 1689 the foundations of the new building were dug. The architect intended leaving nothing except the Tudor Great Hall, but Mary's death in 1694 meant that a wholesale rebuilding of the remaining area was abandoned; what he accomplished was the Park Block and the Privy Gate Block, which together formed two sides of Fountain Court. This building, in the Classical Renaissance style, in red brick and Portland stone admirably matched the old Tudor work.

The fact that William and Mary were joint sovereigns dictated the main features of Wren's state apartments. There had to be a King's Staircase *and* a Queen's Staircase; and this duplication runs throughout the apartments—the King's rooms lying along the south side of Fountain Court, the Queen's along the east, all on the first floor. The apartments were lavishly decorated; indeed, by William's own death the interior was far from complete, though Tijou had already beautified the King's Staircase with a wrought-iron balustrade and Verrio had begun painting the walls and ceiling with scenes from classical mythology.

After George III had come to the throne he never set foot in Hampton Court again, for his grandfather, George II, had once boxed his ears in the state apartments for some innocent remark, and he always connected Hampton with that degrading incident. No succeeding monarch has ever lived there and the Palace became divided into some fifty 'grace and favour' residences, chiefly for the widows or children of those who had given distinguished service to the Crown at Court or in the armed forces. The first occupant of Wolsey's rooms was the widow of Colonel William Crosby who had been Governor of New York. Gradually distinction in other walks of life became a qualification, and a hundred years ago Michael Faraday the scientist was living at Hampton Court, while amongst the occupants of 'grace and favour' residences today is the ballerina Moira Shearer.

Throughout its history the gardens have given the Palace a regal setting. Charles II's head gardener, with the delightful name Rose, succeeded in raising pineapples and for

When William and Mary were captivated by the atmosphere of Hampton Court, 13 miles from the centre of London, they commissioned Sir Christopher Wren (right) to modernize it. His original designs were not approved. However he prepared extensive plans which would eventually have swept away the whole of the Tudor Palace, but when building stopped at the death of Queen Mary the work was only partially finished. The illustrations show Fountain Court (left) and the South Front (right below) as designed by Wren.

a further century his successors enjoyed a special allowance of £100 a year for tending the pineapples at Hampton Court. During the rebuilding of the apartments after the Revolution Mary went to considerable pains to stock the beds and hot-houses with rare plants. She even sent a gardener to Virginia to collect suitable seeds and roots. The charm of the gardens owes much to Lancelot ('Capability') Brown, who was appointed royal gardener in 1750. When he was asked to improve the formal gardens he denied himself the pleasure of changing what he saw and told the King that any 'improvement' would be lacking in taste.

One change 'Capability' Brown did make—that was to plant the vine in a corner of the Old Pond Garden in 1769. If not the biggest vine in Britain, it is the most venerable. It soon reached a remarkable size and by the beginning of the last century was yielding 2,200 bunches of grapes. The main branch is now over 100 feet long. The other outdoor attraction, especially prized today by young children, is the Maze; this was planted at the top of the gardens on the north, which had previously been known as the Wilderness.

St. James's Palace

Once he had acquired Whitehall on Wolsey's fall, Henry VIII wanted to round off the site to the west on which stood the Hospital of St. James in the midst of open fields. In the Middle Ages this had been a religious foundation for leprous women—hence its isolation from the rest of Westminster; but by 1532 the disease had become so mercifully rare that the four inmates enjoying the traditional allowances were all widows, living in what was an exceptionally well-found almshouse. King Henry dissolved the hospital, pensioned off the last inmates and began building a house. The gatehouse with octagonal turrets, designed by John Molton, still stands, with the Tudor Rose and the initials 'H.A.' (for Henry and Anne Boleyn) clearly visible.

The Tudor palace was built round four courts of which Colour Court, Ambassadors' Court and Friary Court remain, though the buildings have been much restored. The Chapel Royal where the Supreme Head of the Church listened for the first time to Tallis' five-part Litany, followed readings from Coverdale's English Bible and heard Cranmer preach, is smaller than most Oxford College chapels. It contains little of the original interior except the ceiling, which is probably the work of Holbein. Henry did not make much use of his new buildings and, indeed, the only Tudor sovereign to live there for any length of time was Mary. She treated it as a private residence in contrast to Whitehall where she held receptions and state ceremonies, and here she died and was buried.

There was little change to the buildings until Inigo Jones began preparing plans for a Roman Catholic Chapel for the use of the Spanish Infanta whom Charles I was

St. James's Palace in 1660, drawn by Hollar, and (right) the same gatehouse today.

St. James's Palace.

St. James's Palace

expected to marry; the match was abandoned, but not the chapel which was completed for Queen Henrietta Maria in 1627—a fine Palladian building, the east end lit by a Venetian window. It was Henrietta Maria who undertook the redecoration and furnishing of St. James's in exquisite taste, and the Tapestry Room is a monument to her patronage of the fine arts. A visitor from the French court thought it 'very magnificent and extremely convenient', though the castellated walls led him to term St. James's a castle. 'To express the great number of chambers, all covered with tapestry and superbly furnished with all manner of furniture . . . would be impossible', for the Palace seemed endless. Nearly all these suites were destroyed by a fire which swept through the east wing in 1809.

Under Charles II, St. James's Park and the Palace gardens were laid out by the French gardener Le Nôtre and the Italian artist Antonio Verrio. The lake was constructed and stocked with water fowl and the Mall laid out and lined with trees. Delighted with all the results Charles opened the Park to the public. The Mall takes its name from the French game of pell mell, akin to croquet, that the King popularized.

Here on June 10, 1688, a date long to be hallowed by Jacobites, was born James, the Old Pretender, and such was the hysterical state of politics that by evening the tale that this was a suppositious child smuggled into St. James's in a warming pan was going the rounds. After Mary II's death in 1694 William III granted apartments in the Palace to Anne and her husband, George of Denmark.

Anne had a special affection for St. James's, where she had been born, and as Queen resided there each autumn and winter. Whitehall was by now a heap of rubble and Greenwich a naval hospital; she could never feel really at home at the palace which her brother-in-law had built at Kensington. Anne's accession consequently opens a new chapter in the history of St. James's. The royal household was more settled than ever before and 'Our Court of St. James's' became synonymous with the sovereign. She added the Banqueting Room and a new range of apartments, including the Throne

An elevation drawing of a proposed scheme by Sir Jeffry Wyatville for 'improving St. James's Palace in a similar manner to his work at Windsor. This drawing was

prepared after the fire of 1809. On the right is Wren's Marlborough House. To the left is Clarence House.

Room, in which she touched little Samuel Johnson, aged two and a half, for the King's evil in 1712. Her Majesty's touch proved ineffective in his case, yet to the end of his days he had 'a confused, but somehow a sort of solemn recollection of a lady in diamonds, and a long black hood'. One of the best additions to St. James's which Queen Anne authorized was the building of Hawksmoor's stable block, with its terminal pavilions, which still stands.

St. James's again became the pivot of society when George II succeeded his father. There were now regular drawing-rooms and levees on Mondays and Fridays and the Queen even received company while she was at her toilet; the door leading to the next room, in which morning prayer was said and sometimes a sermon preached, was left ajar. While Caroline's head-dress was being adjusted 'the conversation turned upon metaphysical subjects, blended with repartees, sallies of mirth and the tittle-tattle of a drawing-room'. But the greatest occasions of the social calendar were the receptions held on the King's and the Queen's Birthdays. On the King's Birthday the Poet Laureate delivered his Birthday Ode before the entire court and then the sovereign watched the parade of mail coaches from the palace windows. Queen Charlotte's Birthday in 1729, the first celebration after the end of court mourning, put a stop to the dullness and dowdyism of the palace. The world of fashion flocked to the levee in the afternoon and the state ball at night. At the levee *débutantes* were presented, one by one: the girls stood still and only the ladies presenting them curtsied to Her Majesty.

When George III settled Buckingham House on his Queen the days of St. James's as a permanent residence for the reigning monarch were numbered. State balls, levees and drawing-rooms were still held and royal marriages and christenings still solemnized in the Chapel there, but the royal family made Buckingham House their London home. For the first time perhaps a proper distinction was made between the sovereign's private and his public life. St. James's remained the headquarters of court ceremonial. Here were to be found the Lord Chamberlain's office and the central chancery of the orders of knighthood; here, too, a stone's throw from the Presence Chamber where the King would receive ambassadors to the Court of St. James's on their first appointment, lived the Marshal of the Diplomatic Corps. The rest of the apartments provided quarters for various household officials and there were even suites of 'grace and favour' residences.

Despite the destruction of so much of the old palace by the fire of 1809, levees were still held in the Throne Room down to 1935. One ceremony always associated with the Chapel Royal at St. James's is the Epiphany offering of gold, which is used for the relief of the poor.

For nearly a century the west wing of the Palace has been known as York House. This was established as a residence for the Prince of Wales and was in due course used by the Duke of Windsor as his London home until his accession. At present the Duke and Duchess of Gloucester live there. It would be difficult to convert the rest of the buildings into comfortable apartments and members of the royal family in recent times have resided at houses built in the old palace ground, such as Marlborough House and Clarence House.

Nonsuch

A unique painting by Henry Danckerts of Nonsuch Palace from the North-East c. 1660. This entrance gives very little idea of the ornate work which confronted visitors to Henry VIII's extravagant mansion. James I thought 'it a lavish place of nonsense'; a sketch made in 1702 shows it in ruins; by 1798 no vestige of the Palace remained.

No man has ever given a house so apt a name as Henry VIII: Nonsuch—None Such; for there was nothing quite like the excessively ornate inner court in the western world and it defied imitation.

> 'That which no equal has in art or fame
> Britons deservedly do Nonsuch name.'

The building of the Palace literally wiped out what had gone before, for the Surrey village of Cuddington which once stood on the site was demolished to make way for Henry's folly; the foundations of Cuddington church and skeletons of bodies buried beneath the chancel were uncovered in the excavations made in 1959. Why should Henry have picked on Cuddington, so near to the existing palaces of Richmond and Hampton Court? Officials and courtiers knew better than to ask the King for reasons. To achieve his whim the writ went forth and the stone church and manor-house, the timbered farmsteads and cottages were no more. In their place was to stand a triumph of fantasy: a splendid mansion with a profusion of turrets and pinnacles, queer clocks and ornate chimney-pots, exquisitely carved slate and bold Parisian plaster casts, the rooms filled with the costly bric-à-brac of majesty. It was more the kind of house that Alice's Red King might have felt at home in than a country house for a king of England.

The building of so costly a place was made possible only by the Dissolution of the Monasteries, which throughout the 1530s were being taken into the King's hands. The religious houses even provided some of the raw materials. On April 13, 1538, Merton Priory was surrendered to the King. A mere ten days later the first cartloads of hundreds of tons of stone were being taken from demolished Merton to Nonsuch. Overnight Merton looked like last year's bird nest. The spade has turned up large chunks of Merton masonry in the palace foundations: a great carved and gilded boss, stones from the pillars, pieces of sculptured angels, fruit and animals that once had been dedicated to the greater glory of God formed the walls of the pleasure dome of the Supreme Head of the Church. Never before had so many craftsmen been concentrated on a building site, for that summer an army of 520 workmen was encamped in tents in what was already being called 'the Park', for King Henry wanted his palace built with as little delay as possible and masons toured as far afield as the West Country and the Midlands impressing labourers, most of whom worked overtime in the summer months.

The Palace was built round two courts, the inner court being entered through a gatehouse and up a flight of steps. The upper section of this inner court was half-timbered and decorated with plaster work of exceptional quality—'garnished with a variety of pictures and other antique forms of excellent arts and workmanship'. The experts attracted to the King's service included William Cure, a carver from Amsterdam, and Giles Gering who directed the intricate plaster work—those statues 'as big as the life' from classical mythology, which so intrigued John Evelyn in the last days of the Palace. The far side of the inner court facing the gardens was formed by a long range of buildings between two octagonal towers and the upper storeys of these were pavilions with countless windows. The pointed leaden roofs were topped by pinnacle and vanes.

Nonsuch

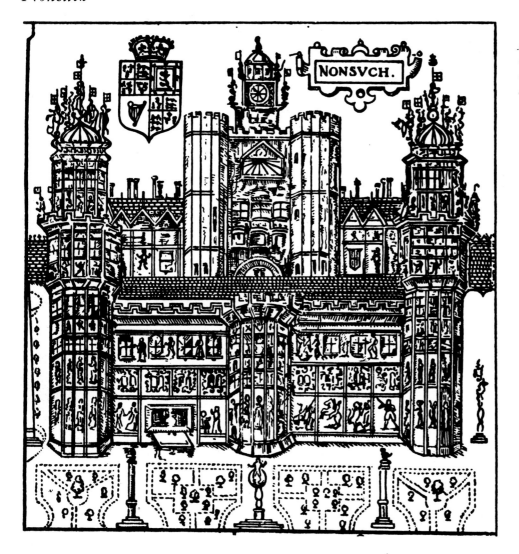

Unique in England, there is good reason for believing that Nonsuch was devised by Henry VIII as a Tudor retort to Francis I's Château of Chambord, which had been begun in the 1520s. Whatever France could accomplish England could outdo. As a foreign visitor noted later in the century: 'One could imagine everything that architecture can perform to have been employed in this one work . . . that it may well claim and justify its name as None Such, being without an equal.' By Henry's death it was still unfinished and had cost £23,000.

Contemporary engravings of the Palace convey the fairy-tale character of the buildings; it was almost as if Henry's architect had been dreaming of the towers of Byzantium. Hoffnagel's drawing gives the impression of a spacious residence set in open country without another roof in sight; but the drawing which John Speed reproduced in a corner of his *Map of Surrey* is probably more reliable, for various important features in it have been corroborated by the evidence of recent archæological finds. The artist's tricks with the law of perspective enable us to look over the roof of the Inner Court to the far side.

Much more than the village of Cuddington suffered. Common lands in several neighbouring parishes were enclosed to make the two parks, totalling some 1,700

To embellish Nonsuch Henry VIII succeeded in securing the services of
Nicholas Bellin of Modena who had worked at Fontainebleau. Bellin
was responsible for the massive stucco reliefs framed in carved slate
which ran round the walls of the Inner Court and along the South front
of the Palace, and these plaster mouldings of a ram's head and a cherub
are fragments of the brilliant work which he inspired.

Nonsuch

Nothing is known to survive of the furniture used at Nonsuch, but this inlaid marble table, illustrated in the Lumley Inventory of 1590, may have been used there during the late 16th century.

acres. These were stocked with 1,000 head of deer for the King's sport—a clear indication that Henry regarded Nonsuch as essentially a hunting-lodge. The banqueting-house was an after-thought. It was not part of the main building, but a timbered structure at the top of the hill in the park where gala picnics were held in the middle of a day's hunting.

Queen Mary never set foot in the place after her accession for it was repugnant to her, largely because it was stamped so unmistakably with her father's personality. She even contemplated pulling down the buildings and selling the estate, but in the event she granted the Palace to Henry Fitz Alan, Earl of Arundel, from whose stepson Queen Elizabeth purchased it in 1591. The first two Stuart kings found the place as eerie and exotic as Prince Albert was to find Brighton Pavilion.

Some feared that the victorious Parliamentary generals would have scant regard for this stately pleasure dome. Yet their surveyors were delighted with the house and gardens and managed to convince their masters that 'this very curious structure' had a considerable market value. The excellence of King Henry's workmanship clearly impressed them and they reported that the plumbing was superb. Nor should the gardens be plundered; the strange trees called 'lilacks', they wrote, bore no fruit but when in bloom were very pretty. Nonsuch was saved and became for ten years the home of a succession of high-ranking army officers—Algernon Sidney, Major-General Lambert and Colonel Thomas Pride, who had led the purge of the House of Commons in 1648. After his mother's death Charles II assigned the place to his mistress, Barbara Villiers. When she fell from power she pulled down what remained of the Palace and sold the park in lots so that the scene closely resembled the destruction of Cuddington village 130 years before.

At last in the long dry summer of 1959 the site of 'the very pearl of the realm' was for the first time thoroughly excavated, and archaeologists traced the foundations of Nonsuch in what was the most extensive operation of its kind on a post-medieval site in Britain.

A survey of Nonsuch undertaken in 1650 refers to 'one fayer fountayne of whyt marble supported with brass dragons under which is a large square cisterne of lead set within a frame of whyte marble.'

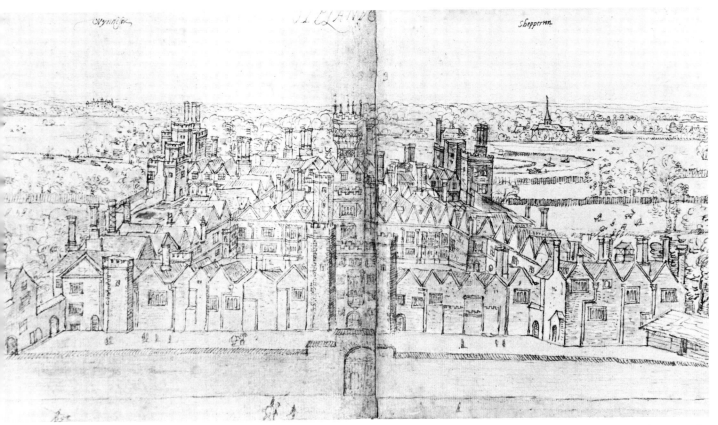

The now vanished manor house of Oatlands, where Queen Anne of Denmark indefatigably experimented with silkworm farming and which, a generation later, became the favourite retreat of her daughter-in-law, Henrietta Maria.

Henry VIII acquired Oatlands, near Weybridge in Surrey, in 1537, because he wanted to add the considerable park that went with the manor house to his honour of Hampton Court. He soon embarked on alterations and here, in July 1540, he married Catherine Howard. But Oatlands was too far from London and too small a residence for more than occasional use and for the rest of the century royal visits were confined to hunting expeditions and a night's stay on progress.

Anne of Denmark was assigned the house as part of her jointure and instructed Inigo Jones to plan improvements. He built a splendid gateway in 1617 and much later added fireplaces and a balcony. But the chief work undertaken at Oatlands at this time was the brick silk-worm house, built in the middle of a spacious mulberry garden. Its staircase was richly ornamented with walls panelled and the windows painted with Queen Anne's arms; yet the silkworms did not appreciate their palatial surroundings and the project, so dear to the Queen's heart, was abandoned.

Henrietta Maria was charmed by Oatlands and frequently visited it each summer with her children. Here in July 1540, exactly a century after Henry VIII's hapless fifth marriage, she gave birth to her youngest son, Henry of Oatlands, for she had decided that Whitehall Palace was no place for a confinement while the constitutional crisis split court and capital. Oatlands was restored to her on her return but she found the house would need extensive repairs. With her children grown up, she no longer needed a place in the country and she leased it to her chamberlain, Henry Jermyn, Earl of St. Albans, whom malicious folk averred was more of a husband than a chamberlain. Before very long the remains of the old palace were pulled down and Oatlands Park, true to its name, reverted to arable farming.

Hatfield House

The Great Hall of the old palace of Hatfield

The medieval bishops of Ely had maintained a manor-house at Hatfield in Hertfordshire where they frequently entertained royal guests on hunting expeditions. This residence had been extensively rebuilt in brick by Bishop Morton, in 1480, around a spacious quadrangle on the lower slope of the hill just to the east of the parish church. To the north were orchards, ornamental gardens and a great park. In time the house was leased to Henry VIII's farrier who found the King became a frequent visitor; and in 1538 Henry decided to acquire the buildings and park by exchanging former monastic property in East Anglia with the Bishop of Ely. Hatfield became in consequence a safe nursery for the royal children, away from the infections and political disaffection so rife in London and Westminster. Eighteen years earlier Henry had also bought neighbouring Hunsdon House.

Princess Elizabeth was granted the house in 1550 and spent the greater part of her sister's reign here. Soon after her accession she granted Hunsdon to her first cousin, Henry Carey, whom she created Lord Hunsdon, but although she rarely returned to Hatfield she still maintained it. In 1607, after a mere sixty-nine years as a palace, James I exchanged Hatfield House for Theobalds, with Robert Cecil, Earl of Salisbury. The Earl replaced Morton's house with an imposing mansion, on the plan of an inverted U, on higher ground, and this has remained the home of the Cecil family ever since.

3   *The House of Stuart*

When James VI of Scotland journeyed south in 1603 to succeed Queen Elizabeth I he was amazed at the splendour of Whitehall and at the numbers of fine houses belonging to the crown of England, which contrasted very markedly with his austere patrimony in his northern Kingdom. Falkland Palace was then in a poor state of repair and, with the exception of Holyroodhouse, the King of Scotland lived in bleak, medieval castles, whereas England, wealthy and in the vanguard of architectural development, could provide for its sovereign right royally. A passionate follower of the chase, James VI and I soon exchanged Hatfield House for Theobalds, for the hunting was better there. He settled Somerset House on Queen Anne of Denmark and (as we have seen) spent considerable sums on her developments at Greenwich and his own new buildings at Whitehall. Charles I no more than continued the various projects begun by Inigo Jones for his father and mother.

Regular maintenance of the royal houses ceased with the coming of the Civil War and when Charles II was restored in 1660 he found few of his residences outside London habitable. Eager for a new country house, he acquired Audley End and, at the end of his reign, entrusted Sir Christopher Wren to build him a palace at Winchester, but James II recalled the architect to undertake new works at Whitehall. After the Revolution of 1688, William and Mary purchased Kensington for their principal London home, while major alterations were being made to Hampton Court. Kensington became even more important with the destruction of Whitehall by fire in 1698, but under Queen Anne, the last of the Stuarts, St. James's again returned to favour.

Somerset House

Somerset / *la* **Maison**

House. / *de* SOMERSET.

Somerset House, drawn by Leonard Knyff. The elaborate gateway, which fronted on to the Strand, can be seen in the background. Nothing now remains of the ancient palace which was entirely replaced in 1776–80 by a building designed by Sir William Chambers to be used as government offices.

Though a Tudor house by origin, Somerset House came into its own as the principal residence successively of the consorts of James I and Charles I, who considerably enlarged it and made it one of the finest homes in Europe. During the turmoil of the Reformation the buildings of London had been transformed, as former ecclesiastical property made way for town residences for statesmen and officials who were increasingly obliged to be in the capital. The most sought after locality was the Strand, the highway linking the City with Westminster—especially the south side which had access to the Thames. The names of the nobles—Burghley, Norfolk, Howard, Exeter, Essex and Southampton—are commemorated in the side streets, though their mansions have long since vanished; and the largest group of buildings in the Strand is still called Somerset House after the duke whose exceptional position and wealth enabled him to create this splendid piece of secular domestic architecture.

Edward Seymour, Duke of Somerset, who seized power as Lord Protector on Henry VIII's death, ordered for himself a superb residence in the area where the bishops of Worcester and Chester had their houses, then surrounded by clusters of mean tenements. Somerset entrusted the building to his steward, Sir John Thynne, 'an ingenious man', who was later to design Longleat in Wiltshire for his own use. Ranged round a quadrangle he constructed a two-storey building in the classical style, with columns and an ornamental parapet. An interesting feature was the two-storey window units, but the glory of the building was the raised gateway on to the Strand, with its 'triumphal arch', executed by William Cure, the stone-carver who had worked on Nonsuch for Henry VIII.

Though French influence has been detected from the extant drawings, the materials were local. Most of the stone was filched from the great cloister on the north side of Old St. Paul's, which contained a representation of 'the Dance of Death' and from the Priory church at Clerkenwell. The duke's workmen had tried to loot stone from St. Margaret's church, Westminster, but were repelled by armed parishioners. Even though so many materials had cost him nothing, Somerset spent a fortune on his house, which remained unfinished on his execution in 1552.

Queen Elizabeth made little use of the house and it became an annexe to Whitehall providing accommodation for courtiers and officials who were entitled to rooms at court. Out of charity the Queen allowed the son of the Duke who had built it to reside in the principal suite.

Under James I the Palace took on a fresh lease of life, for it was granted, together with Oatlands, to Queen Anne of Denmark and by royal command the name was changed to Denmark House. For most of her life in England Anne resided apart from her husband at her principal dower-house; and when Henrietta Maria in turn acquired the building as part of her jointure the name Denmark House remained.

Henrietta Maria soon commissioned Inigo Jones to prepare plans for extensive alterations, though it was not until 1635 that she had sufficient money to begin work on her great chapel. The first Roman Catholic Queen since Mary Tudor, she decided to make the chapel at her dower-house in the Strand a building of exceptional beauty. In the old tennis-court, its floor strewn with flowers, she laid the foundation stone of her masterpiece. It measured 104 feet by 36 feet and cost £5,050. At the west end was

Somerset House

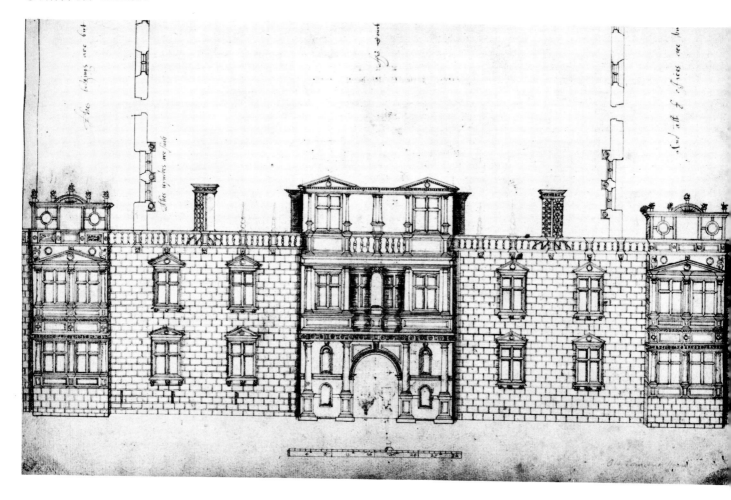

her own closet, a gallery on columns, looking towards the high altar over which was a representation of the Glory of Heaven. The rites of consecration took a full three days and to Henrietta's delight her chapel soon became the regular resort of English Catholics in London.

Henrietta's masques in the hall of Somerset House gave almost as much offence to Puritans as her religion. The trouble was she not only 'overturned morality' by allowing women (instead of boys) to act women's parts in her theatricals, but even dared to appear on the stage herself. The day following an exceptionally splendid royal performance, Prynne published a pamphlet asking how any Christian woman could be 'so more than whorishly impudent as to act, to speak publicly on a stage (perchance in man's apparel and cut hair) in the presence of sundry men and women'.

During the Civil War and Interregnum maintenance ceased and there was talk of demolishing the buildings. A reprieve came with Cromwell's death for it was decided that his remains should lie in state for two months in the former Presence Chamber.

Assured of an income of £60,000 a year on her son's Restoration, Henrietta Maria set about rebuilding Somerset House in the grand manner. Repairs to make good the neglect of twenty years had been completed by November 1662 when the poet Abraham Cowley, the Queen Mother's Secretary of some years' standing, duly produced an ode for her return: Her House now

'Ev'n with the proudest palaces compares.'

A rare architectural drawing from the Elizabethan period by the lesser-known architect John Thorpe (1563–1655). It shows his design for the Strand Gateway of Somerset House, which was demolished about 1775.

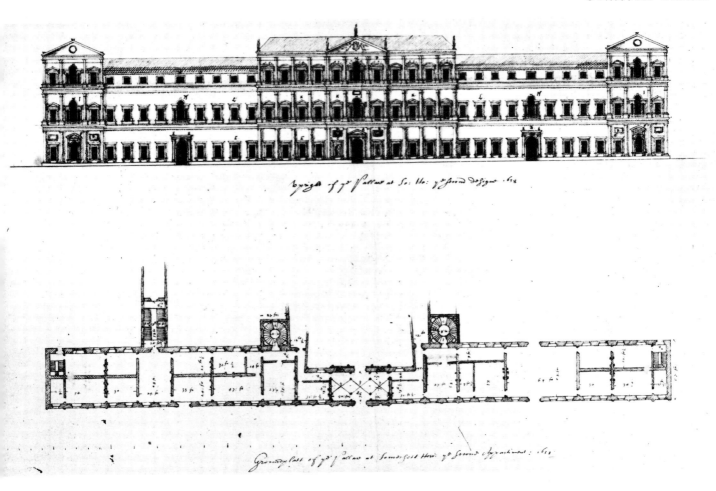

John Webb's drawing of 1638 of the Strand front of a monumental scheme by Inigo Jones to rebuild Somerset House.

Yet making it habitable was but a beginning. She pored over the plans that Inigo Jones had prepared, before the clouds of Civil War had gathered, for making the waterside residence as attractive as any Venetian palace, and decided in the main to follow them; Jones, alas, had died. The frontage on the Strand was adorned with ornate columns and a new gateway led to a spacious quadrangle. The Long Gallery went steadily forward, its windows giving a splendid view of the river and there was, of course, an Italian garden with paved walks and fountains, leading right down to the Thames, through a water gate that was supported by statues of Thames and Isis.

With exquisite taste Henrietta superintended the interior decoration. No item of furniture that was not absolutely first-class would satisfy her. Most of the furniture in her apartment was covered with gilded leather; painted screens that had come from India and beyond kept out the draught. She salvaged what she could of Charles's pictures that had been sold for a pittance after his execution and the floors of her rooms were just as remarkable as the walls; inlaid floors of wood in contrasting colours, which she had selected, were talked about as much as the echo on the great staircase and set a new fashion in elegance. Gilt chandeliers hung from the stuccoed ceiling of the Queen Mother's Presence Chamber. Pepys summed up the renovations as 'magnificent and costly', yet even he had never ventured into the holy of holies. The octagonal dressing-room had panels covered with frescoed figures picked out in gold and a wonderfully domed roof. Another octagonal room led from it—the bathroom,

Somerset House

lined entirely with marble where there were hot and cold bathing-closets. The altar of the redecorated Chapel, tended by Capuchins, shone with plate and vessels that had once belonged to Cardinal Richelieu; this was a timely gift from the Cardinal's niece to replace the altar plate which Henrietta had had to pawn in her days of exile during the time of the Commonwealth.

Fashionable London flocked to Somerset House to pay court to *Madame la Mère* and admire her palace. In her widowhood concerts in the hall arranged by her organist, Matthew Locke, took the place of the masques of old; and Thames watermen would rest on their oars to hear the strains of Lully floating out to them from the great windows.

On Henrietta's death in 1669, her son's consort, Queen Catherine of Braganza, could at last acquire the palace. She was still living in Somerset House at the Revolution of 1688, and as godmother to the Old Pretender she was asked to leave England. When she declined William III did his best to reduce her large establishment and succeeded in limiting her Roman Catholic servants to eighteen. At last in 1692 she returned to her native Portugal to live in a new palace at Bemposta, close to Lisbon. Though Somerset House remained for another eighty-six years as part of the royal jointure, no queen consort again resided there and it became a block of 'grace and favour' residences, chiefly for officers' widows.

Following her marriage to George III, Queen Charlotte inspected Somerset House but pronounced it to be most unsatisfactory, and by Act of Parliament she was

Somerset House. A view of the courtyard in the 18th century.

assigned Buckingham House in its place. Adequate 'grace and favour' apartments were by now available at Hampton Court and so the House in the Strand was demolished to make way for public offices, designed by Sir William Chambers, who partially imitated the work of the Restoration Gallery in the Strand front of the new building. For half a century room was found in Chambers' buildings for the Royal Academy, the Royal Society and the Society of Antiquaries, until they all moved to Burlington House. The site is now occupied by the Board of Inland Revenue, the Registrar General and the Principal Probate Registry. Additions to the new Somerset House, including the east wing built for King's College, have changed the site beyond all recognition.

Theobalds in Hertfordshire, about nine miles from Hatfield, became a royal palace in 1607. The original pronunciation was 'Tibbalds', like the London road of the same name, but only a few purists follow the tradition. The Elizabethan statesman William Cecil had acquired the estate for his second son, hunchback Robert, in 1564 and had soon begun extending the old moated manor house, but within ten years he had replaced it by a splendid residence. The Lord Treasurer had spent vast sums on his 'folly', as he called it. He had begun it 'with a mean measure, but increased by occasion of Her Majesty's often coming'. The mansion ranked as one of the finest architectural adventures of the century and was built around five connecting courtyards. Middle Court boasted a Green Gallery over a seven-arch loggia with the walls painted with a great map of England, while Fountain Court, the heart of the building, was resplendent with a Great Gallery and turretted towers. The gardens were as delightful as the buildings and Queen Elizabeth spoke in high praise of Cecil's 'most stately home', staying here on ten different occasions.

Journeying from Edinburgh at the beginning of his reign, James I stayed four days at Theobalds as Robert Cecil's guest and was amazed at the splendour of the mansion. He was always returning here, for his own country houses seemed poor in comparison. Hints were dropped and Cecil, eager to ingratiate himself with the King, agreed to an exchange of property. James could have Theobalds in return for Hatfield House and various Crown lands in Hertfordshire. The formal surrender of Theobalds in May 1607 was an occasion for great celebrations which included a masque specially written by Ben Jonson.

Despite the addition of new kitchens, some thought Theobalds was not what it had been under the Cecils and complained that Scottish courtiers were making it into a pigsty. Once James had enclosed the park and stocked it with 1,000 head of deer he made frequent use of Theobalds and decorated the walls of the galleries with antlers. It was here, at his favourite home, that he died.

After Charles I's execution a Baptist major persuaded two fellow officers to join him as partners in buying Theobalds, but they regarded the palace largely as a quarry for building materials. What remained of the mansion became settled on General Monck at the Restoration, but soon, like Oatlands and Nonsuch, all was in ruins. The mansion now known as Old Palace House was built as recently as 1768 and nothing remains of Cecil's folly except the garden walls.

Edinburgh Castle

Edinburgh Castle

Many centuries before Queen Victoria discovered Deeside the Kingdom of Scotland supported six royal homes, two of which, Edinburgh Castle and Holyroodhouse, were in the capital. The most ancient house was Linlithgow, fifteen miles west of Edinburgh. In medieval times Parliaments had met within its walls; here Mary Queen of Scots was born. Her son in 1617 ordered William Wallace to carry out extensive renovations but in its last days Linlithgow was reduced to a barracks and the entire palace went up in flames during the Forty-five. James VI, like many of his predecessors, had been crowned at Stirling, a palace within a great fortress that commanded the River Forth, but already by 1583 the royal apartments were very 'ruinous', with the roofs leaking. James V had built a palace at Falkland on the site of an ancient castle and the French workmen who laboured on the courtyard front in 1539 helped to make the palace the first Renaissance building of significance to be constructed in Scotland. But the turbulence of Scottish politics during the crisis of the Reformation, coupled with the Crown's lack of funds, played havoc with the upkeep of Falkland. Within a generation of its completion two galleries were unsafe, the interior woodwork of the King's chamber was rotting and the great hall was about to collapse. The last palace of note, and the only one in the west of Scotland, Dumbarton in Strathclyde, was in no better shape and was a ruin by the time James VI came to the English throne.

Built on a rugged rock 440 feet above sea-level, the Castle was to Edinburgh what the Tower had been to London. It was not only a palace but also a treasury, a strong-room for the Honours of Scotland (the crown jewels), a barracks and an arsenal. Frequent minorities down the years, with rival factions quarrelling for the possession of the King, made the Castle alternately a prison and a place of refuge. It was a key fortress throughout the endemic warfare between England and Scotland and its capture, occupation and recapture punctuate the history of those campaigns of long ago.

The oldest part of the citadel is the chapel built by Queen Margaret at the time when the Norman Conquerors were building the Tower of London. Another Queen Margaret, the daughter of Henry III of England, who came to Edinburgh as a child bride, thought the apartments high on the Rock bleak in comparison with the rooms to which she had been accustomed at Westminster. The Castle was, she said, 'a sad and solitary place, without verdure and, by reason of its vicinity to the sea, unwholesome'.

The Great Hall was built by James IV, but has suffered in its time from military occupation as a barracks and a hospital. The timbered roof and stone corbels are still well preserved and there are carvings on the corbels which relate to James and his Queen, Margaret Tudor, daughter of Henry VII.

Much rebuilding went on during the fifteenth century at the south of the citadel when the King's Lodging was built, but the modern visitor to this suite, which now houses the Scottish United Services Museum, will find little to remind him that this

Little remains of the original fortress of Edinburgh Castle, which has played such a decisive role in its turbulent history, but this photograph shows the formidable site it occupies.

Edinburgh Castle

was once a palace. To the south of it, however, in an older building is the tiny, irregular room in which Mary Queen of Scots in 1566 gave birth to her son who was destined to become the first King of the three Kingdoms of England, Scotland and Ireland. She had wanted her child to be born at Holyroodhouse but her Privy Council had entreated her to remain in the Castle. The omens were propitious, for it was St. Margaret's Day, when Mons Meg, the famous gun that was already a venerable antique, fired a royal salute from the ramparts to honour the baby prince.

Mary paid one last visit to the Castle, just before her fatal marriage to Bothwell, two years later, that led to her abdication, exile and execution; and it was from her apartments in the Castle that the spurious Casket Letters, attempting to prove her complicity in Darnley's murder, were 'discovered' by the Earl of Morton, who as Regent was to build a new gateway to the Castle in 1574.

When James VI became of age he had had enough of forced residence in castles and thereafter he rarely stayed in the apartments in Edinburgh. The carvings in his chamber specially executed for his 'hame coming' in 1617, when £25,000 was spent on renovating the Castle, were erased with older Stuart monograms by Oliver Cromwell, after the siege. Under Charles II the buildings were extensively repaired. Today the Castle comes into its own at the Edinburgh International Festival as the setting for the military tattoo.

(Right, above). St. Margaret's Chapel, built by Queen Margaret, the wife of Malcolm III and the great-niece of Edward the Confessor, in the 11th century. Beyond is the Castle's famous 15th-century cannon.

(Right). The battlements of Edinburgh Castle, with the modern city spread out below and Arthur's seat in the background.

Left). Mary, Queen of Scots' Bedchamber, where the assassination of her Italian secretary, David Rizzio, was carried out by her husband Lord Darnley and others on March 9, 1566.

A royal mile away from Edinburgh Castle lies the Palace of Holyroodhouse, west of the site of an abbey anciently founded by Queen Margaret to house what she believed was a fragment of the True Cross. Down the years Scottish kings and queens had often stayed at Holyrood Abbey guest house, and James II had in turn been born, crowned, married and buried within the abbey precincts. James IV decided to build a palace nearby and when Margaret Tudor came to Edinburgh in 1503 as his bride the house was well advanced. After his death at Flodden, the building continued during his son's minority until the English invasion in 1543 when the commander's orders had been to 'do his best without long tarrying to beat down the Castle and sack Holyroodhouse'. The Palace went up in flames, though the thickness of the walls saved it from utter devastation.

When Mary Queen of Scots returned to Edinburgh in 1560 there was a newly-built palace ready for her and here five years later she married Lord Darnley. During a palace revolution on March 9, 1566, the favourite Rizzio was murdered outside the

Holyroodhouse

Queen's bedchamber and his body was dragged to a spot (now marked by a tablet) near the door of the audience chamber. Soon after her fateful marriage to Bothwell, Mary left Holyroodhouse for the last time; James VI, her infant son by Darnley, was at Stirling Castle when his mother abdicated and he did not enter Holyrood until his coming of age. After his accession in England he returned only once to his native country.

It was not until the eighth year of his reign that Charles I crossed north of the Border to be crowned King. His second and last visit to Holyroodhouse was in 1641 during the Second Bishops' War, provoked by forcing an English Prayer Book on the Scottish Kirk. It was left to Charles II to become the second founder of Holyrood, on the basis of plans drawn up by John Mylne. The west front, which had been hastily rebuilt by Oliver Cromwell after a fire, was demolished to make way for a splendid residence and in 1671 Sir William Bruce laid the foundation stone of the new block, instructing Robert Mylne, John's nephew, to build 'in pillar work' conforming 'with the Doric and Ionic orders'. The south-western tower characteristically balanced the surviving tower of James IV on the opposite side. Charles II never had the satisfaction of spending a single night in the new apartments.

When Bonnie Prince Charlie took Edinburgh without losing a man in the early stages of the Fifty-five he made for the home of his forefathers. Wearing the Stuart tartan, with a velvet bonnet fringed with gold lace, he chose a route to Holyroodhouse out of range of the cannon from the Castle on September 17. At the entrance to the Palace James Hepburn of Keith drew his sword to usher the last of the Stuarts into Holyrood. Later in the day the heralds mustered at the market cross to proclaim his father as James III and VIII and himself as Prince Regent.

A few days later, having routed Cope's army at Prestonpans, Prince Charles led his Highland following in triumph to Edinburgh, with the bagpipes playing 'When the King enjoys His Own again'. That evening he held a state ball at Holyroodhouse, where Jacobite toasts were drunk in usquebaugh, to which he was partial. With the failure of the rebellion the Palace lay neglected.

George IV visited Scotland in 1822, when all the arrangements were made by Sir Walter Scott. Viewing Holyroodhouse in Highland costume, he urged that the Palace should be put in repair, yet when Queen Victoria came there twenty years later the state apartments were quite uninhabitable. There was a rush to get the Throne Room ready for an afternoon reception and then, perhaps mercifully, fears of a scarlet-fever epidemic led to the function being transferred to Dalkeith. She thought the Palace 'a princely and most beautiful place', but spent her time as a guest at Dalkeith and Scone Palaces, long the property of Scottish peers. Yet the ice was broken and long overdue renovations were begun. When Victoria returned with the Prince Consort for a state visit in 1852 they were able to sleep within the walls of Holyrood.

The modern restoration of Holyroodhouse owes much to Queen Mary who personally supervised the redecorations, the choice of furnishings and the hanging of the pictures. That it appears so charming a residence to the modern visitor is a result of her exquisite taste.

(Top, above). *A 19th-century engraving of Holyroodhouse.*

(Above). *The Abbey of Holyroodhouse, which was stripped of its lead roof in 1546 by order of Henry VIII in vengeance when the Scottish Parliament entered into alliance with France.*

The West door of the Abbey, which was the scene of the Coronation, marriage and burial of many Scottish kings since its foundation in the 12th century.

Audley End

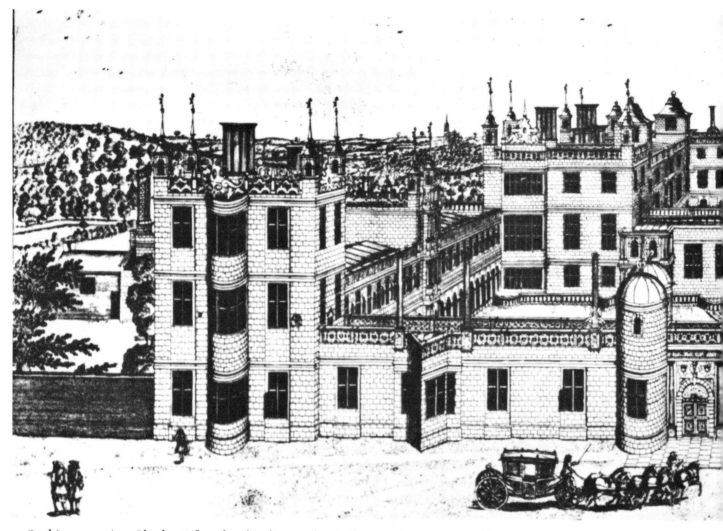

On his restoration Charles II found to his dismay that he had far fewer inhabitable houses than any of his predecessors. Eighteen years of neglect had left many of the royal homes in London and the provinces in a tumble-down state while he was on his travels, and his mother's return to England deprived him of the three houses belonging to her jointure. 'The ancient houses of the Crown having been in great part demolished during the late times', as a courtier summed up the position, Charles made inquiries about a suitable country residence and soon decided upon Audley End, a splendid Jacobean mansion some forty miles north of London, on the Essex-Cambridgeshire borders.

Audley End had been built by Thomas, Earl of Suffolk, between 1603 and 1616 at the astounding cost of £190,000, and was being termed a palace long before King Charles set eyes on it and confessed his 'great liking'. The house had been designed by Bernard Janssen as a remarkable study in symmetry, and as the visitor approached down the avenue of limes it appeared as a building of limitless size. The wooden model of the house which had been made in Italy itself cost £500. James I on his first visit slyly told Suffolk that it was too large for a king but might suffice for a lord treasurer; and when the Earl was dismissed from the treasurership on a charge of embezzlement no one was surprised.

Winstanley's view of Audley End was drawn in 1676 when the mansion was a royal palace, showing it to be a magnificent and rare example of a great house of the Jacobean period. In the foreground is the entrance courtyard with the Great Gate-

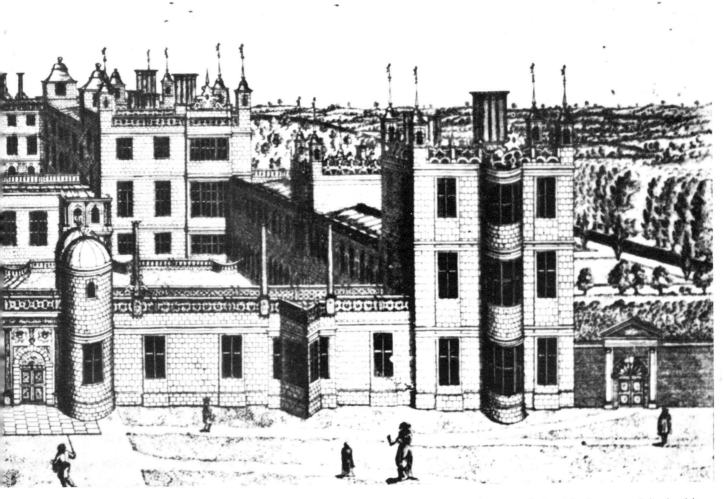

house and its sidewings, enclosing the Base Court, which was demolished on the advice of Sir John Vanbrugh in 1721. Between the two courtyards lies the still surviving Great Hall with its flanking porches.

The great entrance with its four towers has vanished with the rest of the buildings of the first court, but sufficient survives of the second court, including the hall with its splendid screen and panelled ceiling, to show the magnificence of the house which cost Suffolk a fortune and, fifty years on, captivated a king. The apartments were 'full of gaudy, barbarous ornaments', yet the gardens and home park had been laid out in fine taste. The River Cam flowed through the park, while ornamented hills, unusual fountains and other conceits made Audley End a showplace.

The third Earl of Suffolk readily agreed to sell Audley End to the Crown for £50,000, for the upkeep of the great house had been a millstone round his neck. King Charles made full use of the buildings during 1667, and, although no money had passed, Suffolk felt secure for his sovereign appointed him keeper of the palace. Yet as the months went by there seemed no chance that the King would have sufficient funds to complete the purchase. A sum of £2,000 was paid in 1668 and the following year inquiries were discreetly made at the Treasury whether the money voted by a reluctant Parliament for affairs in Ireland could be used towards the Audley debt; something was earmarked from Irish funds, but these paper sums faded fast. Charles found £500 a year for the maintenance of the buildings yet not a penny towards paying off the purchase price. This dragged on to become one of the many bad debts

Audley End

he left behind him, and after the Glorious Revolution the fifth Earl of Suffolk succeeded in regaining his home.

Each spring and autumn Charles II would remove his court to Audley End for a holiday from Whitehall which 'might be cleaned out and put in repair' during his absence. Audley was for him what Sandringham was for George VI. Tennis, pell mell, bowls, the cockpit and the theatre were London pastimes, but at Audley Charles indulged in the sports of a country gentleman; he would be up at dawn for hunting, hawking, coursing hares and, above all, the racing at Newmarket, twenty miles away. He had a small residence at Newmarket but much preferred to stay at Audley.

Here was blessed freedom from affairs of state and the scented languor of Whitehall seemed far away. In place of rigid etiquette there was a riot of informality—'all the jolly blades were racing, dancing, feasting and revelling', wrote one of the party. Even Catherine of Braganza became infected with the happy, informal atmosphere of the Audley End parties. While Old Rowley amused himself with his buckhounds or spread an impromptu feast for the jockeys, the Queen had her own fun, attending Saffron Walden fair disguised as a country lass. Among the guests might be the Indian astrologer Pregnani, who made a showing of picking the winners at Newmarket races, to the Duke of Monmouth's cost. Charles joked to his sister Minette about it: 'He had the ill luck to foretell three times wrong altogether and James believed him so much as he lost his money upon the same.'

Audley End epitomized the most carefree days of the Merry Monarch, and when they were over the mansion ceased to be a royal palace. James II never resided there as King and when the house was returned to the Suffolk family as the only means of cancelling the debt, the fifth Earl found its upkeep an impossible expense. He pulled down the first court and was later glad to sell the estate. For long periods the house which once had rung with royal laughter was unoccupied. In the later eighteenth century children from Saffron Waldron stole the fruit from the orchards and played hide and seek in the long gallery. It was left to the Braybrooke family to preserve what remained of the old palace with fitting dignity. Under the auspices of the Ministry of Works, Audley End is open to the public each summer; the fine collection of pictures on view here today would have delighted King Charles even more than the gardens.

A Wren-Hawksmoor drawing for Charles II's grand palace at Winchester.

Charles II's other departure was to commission Sir Christopher Wren to build a palace at Winchester on the site of the castle, by then in ruins except for the great hall. In earlier centuries royalty had often stayed at the Castle; here Henry I had married Maud of Scotland and here Henry III and, ten generations later, Arthur Tudor had been born. Winchester, like Audley End, was a good centre for country pursuits, but another advantage was that it lay on the Portsmouth road. Once the mayor and corporation caught wind of King Charles's intentions they loyally presented him with the site, 'in case our sovereign lord should think fit to build' upon it, and in March 1683, a year after Chelsea Hospital had been begun, the foundation stone of Winchester Palace was laid.

Both King and architect envisaged a building that was larger and more magnificent than Chelsea, with a great central portico and twin chapels—Anglican balancing Roman Catholic aesthetically and devotionally. But Charles had embarked on building too late in life, and although work proceeded swiftly the building remained unfinished at his death. James II recalled Wren to undertake fresh operations at Whitehall and so Winchester was abandoned. Queen Anne was to bestow the building on her consort, yet no money was forthcoming for completing the work. During the wars of the eighteenth century French prisoners of war were kept here and in the early days of the French Revolution accommodation was found for *émigrées*. Soon English troops were being billeted in the Palace and thereafter it became regularly used as a barracks until its destruction by fire in 1896.

Winchester Palace

Winchester—the Palace that never was. Wren was commissioned to build this new palace for Charles II sited on the hill overlooking this ancient ecclesiastical city. The illustration (above) is an engraving of it as it might have appeared. At Charles' death in 1685 it was incomplete (right), though part of the building was later used as foundations for army barracks.

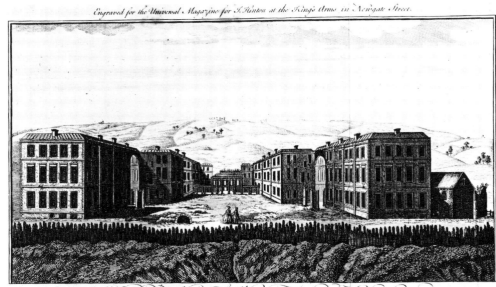

Engraved for the Universal Magazine for I. Hinton at the Kings Arms in Newgate Street.

A Perspective View of WINCHESTER PALACE.

Disappointed with Whitehall and shocked by the lack of comfort at St. James's, William III purchased Nottingham House in Kensington village from his Secretary of State, Daniel Finch, second Earl of Nottingham, for £18,000 soon after the Glorious Revolution. The presence of a gravel pit nearby suggested the house would be eminently suitable for William's constitution, while the beautiful gardens were the chief attraction for his wife.

William and Mary at once ordered Sir Christopher Wen to enlarge the house, and he added four pavilions at the corner of the main block and a two-storied courtyard to the west, entered by a gate-tower. William was impatient to have the house ready for occupation on his return from the war in Ireland and he avidly awaited his wife's reports on the progress of the building. His bedroom, she wrote, smelt of paint and her own apartments were far from ready; the windows were boarded as the scaffolding was still up, and the 'fiddling work' on the outside 'takes up more time than one can imagine'. William was not satisfied and delivered a series of reproofs which Mary abjectly agreed were fully deserved: 'I must needs confess my fault, that I have not been pressing enough till it was too late.' Wren was being forced to carry out these operations with such speed that part of the new building collapsed a matter of minutes after the Queen had left. Yet as early as December 1689 she was able to move in, well aware that the workmen would be busy for many months to come. Their Majesties kept on changing their minds about what they wanted and a fire in November 1691, which destroyed much of the south side of the new courtyard, enabled a more splendid approach to be made to the King's Staircase, for there had to be two quite separate entrances and staircases, one for the King at the west, the other for the Queen at the north, since William and Mary were joint sovereigns.

Because of the more extensive alterations that were undertaken when George I decided to turn his country house into a small palace, Wren's work seems strangely unharmonious and lacking in symmetry. The building remains an architectural

Kensington Palace

hotch-potch (even the clock in Clock Court is not the original but came from dismantled Carlton House). Wren's finest room is undoubtedly the King's Gallery, 96 feet long with great bay windows, in which William hung the finest of his pictures. The original ceiling was plain; the grandiose painting on it of the adventures of Ulysses by William Kent was commissioned when the apartment was no longer a picture gallery. Over the fireplace is a curious wind-dial specially made for King William. The pointer which shows the direction of the prevailing wind is connected by rods to a vane on the roof, and on the dial is painted a map of north-west Europe, its pivot being Kensington. This dial fascinated the old campaigner.

By the time of Anne's accession Kensington village had become the most fashionable residential site in the London area. Anne herself disliked the Palace at first, as it was too identified with her brother-in-law, whom she had loathed. But because it was a 'twin palace', with King's and Queen's apartments of equal dignity, this meant that Anne could live regally in Mary's quarters and need never set foot in the rooms inhabited by Dutch William. She talked much of adding to the buildings, as they proved far too small with the loss of accommodation after the great fire at Whitehall, yet she did no more than have the gardens laid out and the orangery (originally a brick greenhouse) built by Nicholas Hawksmoor, with circular domes at each end.

George I was prepared to live at Kensington provided it were enlarged, and William Benson built—rather too hastily—an additional suite. Soon afterwards it was necessary to reinforce these, and the core of the building (old Nottingham House) was found to be in a ruinous state so it was now replaced by the Cupola Room with drawing-rooms on either side. Wren had been deprived of his post and the work was entrusted to Sir John Vanbrugh, while William Kent was to direct the interior decoration. The King's Staircase that Wren had built for William III seemed to George I to be little better than a backstairs to a palace, and he ordered its transformation into a Grand Staircase that would lead to an ornate Presence Chamber. The windows were altered, the panelling removed and the landing at the top extended. There was no master to continue Tijou's splendid wrought-iron balustrade and the final section of it that was now added shows a notable falling-off in craftsmanship. Yet the walls and ceilings painted by Kent undoubtedly made it an imposing entrance. From a marble balustrade groups of people look out over the stairs to welcome the sovereign and some of the figures were easily indentified, including the artist and an actress he loved.

For all the improvements to the buildings everyone thought the gardens more splendid than the house. The orderly arrangement of flowers and shrubs with gravel walks between clipped hedges that William III had ordained was transformed by Henry Wise, Queen Anne's gardener. The gravel pit that had attracted Dutch William was swept out of sight: 'It must have been a fine genius for gardening', wrote Addison in the *Spectator*, 'that could have thought of forming such an unsightly hollow into so beautiful an area.' Neat lawns and beds boasting an astonishing variety of plants from Europe and North America made a fine splash of colour. At the end of his reign George I commanded Wise to prepare plans for far-reaching changes which were carried out in the next few years by his successor. The Round Pond was constructed and six separate ponds became the Serpentine; in 1731 two yachts were placed on it

The lovely Orangery, probably the joint work of Vanbrugh and Hawksmoor for which the design was approved by Queen Anne in June 1704.

Kensington Palace

(Left). *Though Kensington Palace houses the London Museum and some of the State Apartments are open to the public, many of the apartments are 'grace-and-favour' residences bestowed on members of the royal household. This photograph shows the home of Princess Margaret and Lord Snowdon.*

for the diversion of the royal family. The earth excavated during these works was used for an ornamental mount—long vanished—planted with evergreens, on the top of which was built a revolving arbour so that Queen Caroline could be sheltered from the wind. To the north of this mount was the Queen's Temple, a more formal summer-house which has since been adapted as a keeper's lodge. Caroline stole some 300 acres from Hyde Park to enlarge Kensington Gardens which she fenced in for her menagerie.

George II, like William and Anne before him, died at Kensington. Thereafter the state rooms were shut up and though they were kept available for the sovereign, should he desire to come into residence, they were deserted for three reigns. The rest of the Palace became divided into apartments for members of the royal family. This played havoc with the interior arrangements of Wren and his successors; extra floors were inserted, grand entrances sealed off. George III granted the south wing to his sixth son, the Duke of Sussex. The first occupant of the two lower floors beneath the state rooms was Edward, Duke of Kent, George III's fourth son; here on May 24, 1819, his daughter, the future Queen Victoria, was born, in what is now Room 22 of the London Museum. Here the Princess spent her childhood under the eagle eyes of her mother and Baroness Lehzen, her tutor. A fortnight after her accession in 1837 she moved into the newly-finished Buckingham Palace, glad to be mistress of her own house, while the Duchess of Kent stayed on at Kensington.

On her mother's death Victoria granted her suite to Princess Mary and her husband, the Duke of Teck, and here was born Princess May, who as Queen Mary was to enrich the state rooms with many gifts from her own incomparable collection of Victoriana. The fact that 'Poor May' had been born in the same bedroom at Kensington endeared her to Queen Victoria. To mark her Golden Jubilee in 1899 the Queen

The rambling old building of Kensington Palace. To the left, standing on its own, is the Orangery, and in the centre is the Dutch sunken garden and lily pond; beyond is Kensington Gardens.

decided to restore the state apartments and open them to the public. As far as possible they have been furnished as they were in her childhood; the wallpaper in the bedroom has even been printed from the original blocks. Pictures, dresses and personal items of her later life have been added to make the bedroom, ante-room and nursery into a veritable Victoria museum.

Later residents of the private apartments have been Princess Alice and the Earl of Athlone, and Princess Beatrice. On her marriage to Lord Snowdon, Princess Margaret was granted the apartments formerly occupied by the Marquess of Carisbrooke. The late Princess Marina's children, the Duke of Kent and Princess Alexandra, also have quarters here, while various suites are kept as 'grace and favour' residences for distinguished servants of the royal household. The rest of the Palace provides accommodation for the London Museum, which richly illustrates the social history and development of the capital from prehistoric times. Various royal items are on display, including the cot used by all her children, grandchildren and great-grandchildren (in England) of Queen Victoria.

Marlborough House

Extends 125.

a Scale of 60 Feet.

In the days of her pre-eminence Sarah, Duchess of Marlborough had won from Queen Anne the gift of a royal plot in Pall Mall and here, on May 24, 1709, she laid the foundation stone of Marlborough House. She entrusted the building to Sir Christopher Wren who erected a two-storey red-brick house, comprising a rectangular block with wings at the east and west and a courtyard to the north. Blenheim Palace at Woodstock was to be the nation's gift to her husband, but Marlborough House she considered was her memorial. When the first Lady of the Bedchamber fell from power, through the intrigues of Harley and St. John, Duchess Sarah ransacked her apartments at St. James's Palace, bringing with her all the fittings capable of removal—even door-knobs and panels were taken away for ultimate use at Marlborough House. She commissioned Laguerre to paint battle-scenes featuring her husband and on the staircase he depicted episodes from Ramillies and in the saloon the glories of Blenheim, with the Duke taking Marshal Tallard's surrender.

The house remained in the Churchill family until 1817 when it passed to the Crown and was assigned to Princess Charlotte (the Prince Regent's daughter) on her marriage

(Above, and above right). The front and the garden elevation of Marlborough House, designed by Sir Christopher Wren as a London home for the Duke and Duchess of Marlborough. It has been much altered since it was built in 1709.

(Right). *Marlborough House Chapel, built by Inigo Jones in 1623–7 as the Queen's Chapel at St. James's. It was originally intended as a Chapel Royal for the Catholic Infanta of Spain whom Prince Charles intended to marry but, when this plan failed, it served the court of Henrietta Maria. It stands today, largely unchanged.*

Marlborough House

Queen Mary resided at Marlborough House from her widowhood in 1936 to her death in 1953. This photograph of her bedroom was taken in the late 1930s.

to Leopold; she died before it was ready for her, but Leopold lived on here until he became King of the Belgians in 1831. For twelve years it was the home of Queen Adelaide, William IV's widow, and on her death was ear-marked for the Prince of Wales, who brought his Danish bride here in 1863. The gay, unorthodox entertainments of Bertie and Alexandra and their circle of friends during the London season earned them the nickname of 'the Marlborough House Set'.

A third storey had been added in the late eighteenth century, but now an attic storey was put on top of this and a new block covering the south side of the courtyard, which completely altered the appearance of Wren's house. Between 1910 and 1924 Marlborough House was again the home of Queen Alexandra, by far the longest single resident, and in the gardens she placed memorials to her pets. Her grandson, the future Duke of Windsor, had little liking for the place, preferring to live in St. James's; but the house again became occupied during Queen Mary's widowhood. In more recent days Marlborough House has become the setting for Commonwealth Prime Ministers' conferences.

4　The Hanoverians & After

Exactly a century spans George III's purchase of Buckingham House (in 1762) and the Prince of Wales' acquisition of Sandringham (1862). Early in those years Kew Palace became the country retreat of the royal family and soon the Prince Regent built Carlton House and Brighton Pavilion for his own delights and, as King, re-designed Buckingham Palace and the state apartments at Windsor Castle; while a generation later Queen Victoria and the Prince Regent bought themselves holiday homes at Osborne in the Isle of Wight, and at Balmoral. This represents a hundred years of very considerable activity for architects and builders, but since 1862 there has been little change. Queen Victoria presented Kew to the nation and her son similarly gave her house at Osborne, but there have been no new royal homes. In the intervening century tradition has hardened so that Her Majesty today has the same official residences in England and Scotland, in her public role as sovereign, as her grandfather enjoyed and the same two private houses, Sandringham and Balmoral.

Buckingham Palace

Goring House, as drawn on a fan, was the first house built on the site of Buckingham Palace. It was burnt down in 1674.

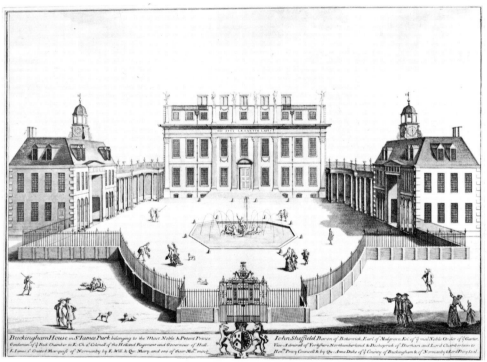

Buckingham House, built by William Winde in 1703. It was considered one of the sights of London and was the prototype of many English country houses of the early 18th century. The façade was remodelled by William Chambers in 1765 and the house was demolished in 1825.

The garden (south) front of Buckingham Palace as built by John Nash in 1825–30. It proved to be a vastly expensive undertaking for which the King was heavily criticized. Nash was finally dismissed, but much of his façade still remains.

Her Majesty's principal residence has been Crown property for less than two centuries and, since the building was acquired as a private family house, it was a long time before it became designated a palace. After the birth of their eldest child, George III and Queen Charlotte decided that St. James's made a most inconvenient London home; and looking round for a suitable house that stood amidst extensive gardens, they soon settled on Buckingham House, built by John Sheffield, Duke of Buckingham, at the beginning of the eighteenth century and in 1762 owned by Sir Charles Sheffield who agreed to part with it for £28,000. It was still called Buckingham House for another dozen years until it became assigned to Queen Charlotte as a dower house, by Act of Parliament, in place of Somerset House, which she had surrendered: henceforth it was known as 'the Queen's House'. On George IV's accession the name was changed to 'the King's House, Pimlico', and it was only when Nash's extensive alterations were in progress that people started calling it a palace—at first 'the New Palace in St. James's Park', and then Buckingham Palace.

The northern part of the site had been set aside by James I for a mulberry garden for silkworms and here the first keeper planted 30,000 mulberry trees. On the eve of the Civil War, when it was abundantly clear that the royal silk industry could never be revived, Lord Goring acquired the post of Keeper of the Mulberry Gardens in order to erect a twenty-room house to the south of it on waste land taken in from the Park. During the Interregnum Goring House was for a time the home of Speaker Lenthall, but the Mulberry Gardens became a pleasure ground. Part was used as a bowling alley, part was turned into an orchard and the rest was planted with whitethorn 'in the manner of a wilderness or maze walk'. When the Puritans closed Spring Gardens as a sink of iniquity the Mulberry Gardens came into favour as the chief open-air spot where London amused itself—'the only place of refreshment about the town for persons of the best quality to be exceedingly cheated at', as Evelyn put it.

When Charles II returned to Whitehall, Lord Goring regained possession of his house, but before long it was sold to Lord Arlington, the Secretary of State; here his duchess brewed the first pot of tea to be made in England. People still called it Goring House but after its destruction by fire in 1674 Arlington House took its place. At the end of the century the house passed to the Duke of Grafton and in 1702 was purchased by John Sheffield, Duke of Buckingham, the patron of Dryden, and for sixty years it remained in the Sheffield family.

Duke John, itching to excel as a patron of taste, pulled down Arlington House and commissioned Captain Winde, a Dutchman, to replace it with a superb building. The new Buckingham House was built slightly to the north of the old mansion and this re-siting, so that the middle of it fronted the central avenue of St. James's Park, gave it a magnificent vista. The great staircase, at the foot of which was a marble statue of Cain and Abel, was one of the wonders of London, and there was a spacious courtyard, leading to gardens laid out by Henry Wise. It was so fine a place that the Duke's widow was asked by the future George II if she would sell it: she would not part with her home for less than £60,000, or lease it at under £3,000 a year, for 'all His Majesty's revenue cannot purchase a place so fit for them', but both Prince and monarch thought it a fantastic sum.

Buckingham Palace

An aquatint of Buckingham Palace from The Microcosm of London, published by Rudolph Ackerman in 1808. The building was drawn by Charles Augustus Pugin while Thomas Rowlandson provided the satirical figures.

The front of Buckingham Palace as designed by Nash. The triumphal arch is now sited at Marble Arch.

Forty years later, on June 6, 1762, George III moved his Queen to this secluded spot. Charlotte was content with modest alterations. When people spoke of 'the sumptuous and stately improvements', they were referring to the interior decorations. For the first time in a royal residence the various suites were called after the colours of the furnishings, and of them all, the Green Closet, the Queen's inner sanctum, was the finest. By the end of her life the Queen's House was no longer the quiet retreat from court ceremonial as it had been fifty years before, for drawing-rooms and other state gatherings had intruded on the Queen's privacy.

When George IV succeeded his father it was assumed that he would continue to live at Carlton House, but after some months of uncertainty he decided to embark on spectacular alterations to what was now 'the King's House'. Sir John Soane proffered carefully prepared plans, but the King remained faithful to his protégé, John Nash, who had rebuilt Brighton Pavilion and Carlton House. 'I am too old to build a Palace', the King told Nash. 'If the Public wish to have a Palace, I have no objection to build one, but I must have a *pied-à-terre*.' So the architect abandoned his scheme for a new home aligned with Pall Mall, yet his transformation of 'the King's House in Pimlico' into Buckingham Palace caused an outcry on the score of expense. The Commons had voted £200,000 'for repairs and fitments' in 1825, on the understanding that they would not be asked for a penny more. Yet it was an open secret that much more than this had already been spent, and in 1828 awkward questions were asked in Parliament about misappropriated funds and the architect's unauthorized extension of his commission. Nash designed a long block in Bath stone, incorporating the chief walls of the old house. Its entrance was in the middle of the east front under a portico and on either side of this portico were columned pavilions. The building was extended eastwards in two low wings, terminating in high pavilions. The dome of the garden block peeped rather incongruously over the central portico and the side pavilions looked distinctly odd and were ordered to be demolished.

At first new stables had gone up and gardens laid out, but now the entire structure of the King's House was being altered. To hide the fact that very extensive operations were in progress from all except those who succeeded in visiting the site, the new walls were exactly the same height as the old and the area of the new Palace the same as before. At last Nash had come into the open with estimates that mentioned 'pulling down the wings forming the quadrangle, rebuilding them further apart and forming a colonnade on each side'. If this was not *rebuilding*, what was it?

M.P.'s voiced their dislike for what they were having to finance. 'Foreign countries might indulge in frippery', thundered the Radical, Joseph Hume, 'but England ought to pride herself on her plainness and simplicity', and he regretted that George IV's tastes in architecture were not 'simple, chaste and solid English'. Another lamented the dome, 'that wretched inverted egg-cup' at the top of Buckingham Palace.

Nash's estimates for works at what he called 'The New Palace in St. James's Park' were again formidable in 1829. The change of name was topical, for to meet attacks in the press on the costly royal building programme it was given out that when Buckingham Palace was complete, St. James's would be demolished. Nash explained that full use was being made of 'best floors, scagliola columns, chimney pieces, slabs

Buckingham Palace

and wood carving' from dismembered Carlton House, though timber, bricks, lead and ordinary flooring from that site 'have not been considered as applicable to the New Palace'. No less than £34,450 was spent on providing a sculptured arch in Ravaccione marble at the grand entrance, between the projecting wings. The triumphal Arch of Constantine at Rome had inspired this massive Marble Arch which was intended as a memorial to the victims of Trafalgar and Waterloo. When the east front of the Palace was begun twenty years later it was removed to its present site at the north-east corner of Hyde Park, an operation costing £11,000 which was paid out of the proceeds of the sale of Brighton Pavilion. George IV would have been more disturbed by the fate of his statue that was to have been placed on top of the Arch. He had ordered Sir Francis Chantrey to make a bronze equestrian statue of himself, but he died before it was finished. After repeated applications by Sir Francis Parliament at last cleared up the bill and decided to place the statue in Trafalgar Square.

Despite Parliament's gloomy verdict, the royal patron thought the building looked splendid, it was so much more than a *pied-à-terre* that he would hold courts in the state-rooms. To hasten his occupation, workmen carried on by candlelight, yet when George died the still unfinished buildings almost suffered the same fate as his father's Gothic Palace at Kew. A committee of architects examined its alleged structural defects in detail and advised on safety precautions. In the end William IV decided against selling the piles of marble and ordered the works to be resumed. The Treasury had already taken advantage of the demise of the Crown to suspend the troublesome Nash from his post as architect to the Board of Works and they closely supervised the expenditure of his successor, Edward Blore, who had come to fame as designer of Sir Walter Scott's Abbotsford. The outside of Buckingham Palace—three sides of a large courtyard, open to the park on the east—was at last complete when the Houses of Parliament were destroyed by fire and King William offered the building to Parliament as a permanent home to replace the Palace of Westminster; after due consideration the offer was gratefully declined. Some still thought the building too small: 'even in the very cast of the rooms of state, if one may be allowed the expression, snugness is evident in the midst of the greatest profusion of splendour'. In the next two years the interior was gradually furnished and the Palace was at long last ready to receive its sovereign when William IV died. It had cost the nation £719,000.

A fortnight after her accession Queen Victoria took the courageous decision of moving from Kensington to Buckingham Palace. Diehard detractors of Nash's building, which had been born amidst such misgivings, made the most of the fact that the first sovereign to sleep within its walls had chosen the thirteenth of the month for her *début*—a most unhappy augury for the future, they pronounced; but the Queen was immune from such shafts. Her first impressions were most favourable: 'I am much pleased with my rooms. They are high, pleasant and cheerful.' Kensington had been her home as a princess and she was glad at last to be in royal apartments some distance from her mother's.

All too soon inconveniences became apparent and urgent alterations were ordered while Victoria was away at Windsor. The Picture Gallery and the Bow Room, were

Edward Blore provided much needed additional rooms for Queen Victoria's Buckingham Palace by building a frontispiece joining the wings. The Builder of 1847 commented that the design 'does not pretend to grandeur and magnificence, scarcely to dignity being 'little more than an ordinary piece of street architecture'.

(Below). Sir Aston Webb prepared this design for refacing the East front in 1912. The remarks such as 'The King is not sure what these are!' and 'The King wants to see details of these figures. It is doubtful whether H.M. will like figures in this position' are written by Lord Esher, his private secretary.

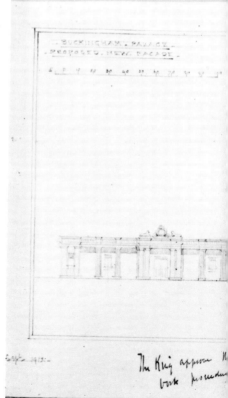

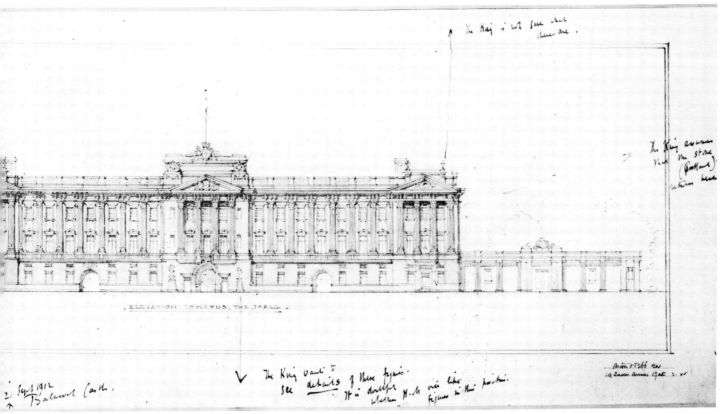

Buckingham Palace now. The figure on the right is a part of the memorial to Queen Victoria erected in 1901.

The Ballroom of Buckingham Palace laid as for a State Banquet in honour of a visiting Head of State. This room, by far the largest of the State Apartments, is where Presentations were formerly made to the Sovereign and where Investitures are held several times a year.

to be properly ventilated; and there must be sinks for the chambermaids on the bedroom floors.

In February 1845, in a letter to her prime minister, the Queen lamented the 'total want of accommodation for our little family, which is fast growing up. Any building must necessarily take some years before it can be safely inhabited. If it were to be begun this autumn, it could hardly be occupied before the Spring of 1848, when the Prince of Wales would be nearly seven and the Princess Royal nearly eight years old, and they cannot possibly be kept in the nursery any longer . . . Independent of this, most parts of the Palace are in a sad state, and will ere long require a further outlay to render them *decent* for the occupation of the Royal Family or any visitors the Queen may have to receive. A room capable of containing a large number of those persons whom the Queen has to invite in the course of the season to balls, concerts, etc., than any of the present apartments can at once hold is most wanted.'

She also insisted on measures being taken to 'render the exterior of the Palace such as

Buckingham Palace

no longer to be a *disgrace* to the country'.

Two years later Sir Edward Blore began building the east front in answer to the Queen's prayer. This completed the quadrangle and sealed off the Palace from the outer world. Victoria had to wait until 1856 for her new ballroom, designed by Sir James Pennethorne, on the site of the original chapel to the south: the south-west conservatory had earlier been consecrated as a new chapel. At last there was a room large enough for entertaining great numbers of guests and Court drawing-rooms were accordingly transferred from St. James's.

Soon after Edward VII's accession extensive changes were made both inside and outside the Palace. He decided that the front of the Palace would be the most fitting place for the memorial to his mother and by a characteristic touch Motherhood was to be included among the virtues represented in the memorial designed by Sir Thomas Brock. Edward did not, however, live to unveil it himself, and by then the vista had changed. A royal entrance was given to the Mall with the building of the Admiralty Arch and its architect, Sir Aston Webb, completed the scene by refacing the east front of the Palace. The stonework there had deteriorated badly and Webb aimed at making his simple façade serve as a backcloth to the Victoria Memorial. The building of the balcony, known to millions the world over, in a masterly way overcame the 'barrier' of the east front which had so completely shut off the Palace. In 1913 King George V entertained at the old Holborn Restaurant the 500 workmen who had just completed the re-facing.

Little has changed externally since then. Very far from being an architectural masterpiece, the Palace owes its majestic appearance to its site and the best way of appreciating it is from an aerial view.

The Grand Hall stands on the same spot as the entrance hall of Buckingham House. To the right is the Marble Hall, to the left the Grand Staircase which Nash built in place of the Duke of Buckingham's painted staircase; it is hung with full-length portraits of royalty of which the most imposing is Wilkie's portrait of the Duke of Sussex. At the head of the Staircase is the long Picture Gallery which was originally designed for George IV's collection chiefly of Dutch masters. Yet every room is a minor gallery, and since 1961 exhibitions of selected royal treasures have been put on display in a small museum for the benefit of the public. The founding fathers of the Palace are appropriately commemorated in the Dining-Room; Lawrence's George IV has pride of place over the mantelpiece, while Gainsborough's portraits of his father and mother look approvingly across the room where one day another King George would give his famous dinners to members of the Jockey Club on Derby Day.

The Blue Drawing-Room (the original ball room) where receptions are held is perhaps the most beautiful room of all. Its ceiling is supported by columns painted to resemble onyx and enriched with gilt capitals while the walls are hung with turquoise. Here is the Table of the Great Commanders which was made for Napoleon in 1812 and subsequently presented by Louis XVIII to the Prince Regent; it is made of Sèvres porcelain, with ormolu mounts and on its circular top are painted the great generals of antiquity. The most interesting object in the music room is not a musical instrument but the clock designed by George III in collaboration with Sir William

Buckingham Palace today which can be compared with the drawing of Nash's West front. The large building on the right is the ballroom added by Sir James Pennethorne in 1853–5.

Chambers. Finally, in the Throne Room, completed in 1833, we may notice the frieze in high relief depicting incidents from the Wars of the Roses, culminating in the marriage of Henry Tudor with Elizabeth of York.

From Buckingham Palace the Queen leaves in the Irish State coach each November to open a new session of Parliament; in the Ball Room she holds a series of investitures, following the New Year and Birthday Honours' Lists and in the summer entertains guests to Garden Parties. In the Palace Her Majesty gives regular audiences to her Prime Minister, is present for the swearing of new Privy Councillors and receives overseas ambassadors and high commissioners on their appointment to the Court of St. James's. Besides the great entertainments arranged to welcome heads of state, there are the informal luncheon parties at which the Queen and her husband meet an increasing number of men and women of distinction from all walks of life.

What prove to be the milestones of each reign bring crowds to the Palace; yet Buckingham Palace is more than a setting for ceremonies, for it is the home of a busy sovereign and her family for the greater part of the year, and it is the Study today, not the Throne Room, that is the hub of the Palace.

Kew Palace

The Palace at Richmond had last been in regular use in the 1630s, and the neighbourhood did not regain royal favour for another century. George II as Prince of Wales had taken Richmond Lodge to get away from his father, and here Queen Caroline set the fashion for grottoes by building Merlin's Cave in the gardens, tended by the rustic poet Stephen Duck. To embarrass the King, Frederick Prince of Wales bought Kew House (or the White Lodge) which had belonged to the astronomer Samuel Molyneux, for it was but a stone's-throw from Richmond Lodge. 'Poor Fred's' widow began the Gothic Revival in English architecture by putting up in the gardens the 'Alambra', a Turkish mosque, a Roman arch and a Gothic cathedral. Sir William Chambers who had executed these fantasies later built the Chinese Pagoda at Kew, still a landmark, for the honeymoon of George III and Queen Charlotte, who delighted in their Surrey retreat.

At first they had lived at Richmond Lodge, but with the death of the dowager Princess of Wales in 1771, they could move into Kew House. As the family grew, other houses on Kew Green, such as the present palace (or Dutch House) were taken over as lodgings. But in 1779 George III lost patience with the local worthies who had refused to sell land he needed for extending the Palace and he shook the dust of the place off his feet for Windsor. He next visited Kew in 1788 with his first attack of madness.

George III suddenly became taken with the idea of building a grandiose Gothic palace by the banks of the Thames. His surveyor-general, who had just redesigned the state apartments at Windsor, prepared plans after the King's heart and as a first step the White House, which blocked the site, was pulled down. While his castellated palace was being built the King moved into the Dutch House (the present Palace), a house designed for a Dutch merchant in 1663. The new venture was to be a kind of late-Georgian Nonsuch. The shell of the building was largely finished when George became blind and then, in 1810, permanently deranged; he stayed on in the Dutch House and the dream palace was never completed. It was too much at variance with the tastes of the Prince Regent who was firmly settled in Brighton Pavilion and Carlton House. Vast sums had been spent on this folly and in 1828 Parliament having looked into the accounts ordered the building to be demolished; such materials as could not be sold were to be used at other royal residences. Much of the flooring and staircases were in fact used by Nash in the rebuilding of Buckingham Palace.

When she came to the throne Queen Victoria gave the greater part of Kew Gardens to the nation. She reserved for her own use Queen's Cottage, Charlotte's favourite summer house, to the south of the estate, where the wedding breakfast of her parents had been held in July 1818. She rarely visited it, and to commemorate her Diamond Jubilee the Queen presented the cottage and its grounds to her subjects. Appropriately for a site re-ordered in the grand style by 'Capability' Brown, it is the Botanical Gardens, rather than the miniature palace of the Dutch House, that arouse interest today.

A model dating from 1735 of an ambitious scheme by the architect William Kent for building a royal palace at Kew.

The modest house at Kew where George III lived with his large family and where George IV was born.

Carlton House

No monarch since Henry VIII has equalled the building programme of George IV. His permanent legacies to the Crown are Buckingham Palace and the state apartments at Windsor; but the town and country houses he built for himself as Prince Regent and continued to use after his accession were every bit as impressive, even though Carlton House has long since disappeared from Pall Mall while Brighton Pavilion ceased to be a royal residence in 1850.

Carleton House (as it was spelt) had been built originally by Henry Boyle, Baron Carleton, on what was once the shrubbery of St. James's Palace. Queen Anne had leased him this plot at a modest rent of £35 a year and his red brick house that fronted the Waterloo Place of today was unostentatious. His nephew, Lord Burlington, who inherited it from him, cased the brickwork with stone, improved the gardens with statuary, and in 1732 sold it to the Countess Dowager of Burlington. Within the year it had been acquired by Frederick, Prince of Wales. Leicester House was his London home but he wanted to have a 'ceremonial house' in the shadow of St. James's where he could embarrass his father by holding receptions and balls. Peers and commoners of the Opposition thronged to these functions until 'Poor Fred' died in 1751. His widow feared she would be turned out of Carlton House by the Prince's creditors or perhaps by the Crown taking over the property; but George II reassured her that her tenancy would not be disturbed and for another twenty-one years she lived quietly in her 'pretty place' during the season.

On his coming of age in 1783 the Prince of Wales was given the freedom of a separate establishment at Carlton House. He deemed it too modest a house and called in Henry Holland, who had recently completed Brook's Club, St. James's Street, the Whig headquarters, to make extensive additions and alterations. The façade was renewed, a Corinthian portico added on the north front and an open colonnade built in front of the courtyard. The interior was remodelled on no less lavish a scale with a series of elegant drawing-rooms, a great ballroom, and, strange novelty, a Chinese Room. The heart of the building was the 'tribune', or ceremonial vestibule. At the end of the Gallery was a temple, furnished with a glass chimney-piece, a clock girandole and more exotic *objets d'art*. With its homage to French taste, inside and out, it was reckoned the finest house in London.

The Prince's alterations to Carlton House were the most costly operations hitherto undertaken at any royal residence, only to be exceeded by his works at Windsor when he became King. In six years his unpaid bills for these improvements reached the dizzy figure of £133,505 and there was another sum of £90,804 owing to tradesmen for personal items. His father asked Parliament to vote this money on the understanding that the Prince had solemnly promised 'to confine his future expenses'. But to alter his style of living the Prince found quite impossible, and a Committee of Enquiry was appointed which made further revelations of reckless expenditure at Carlton House; embellishments were being made to the Gallery, for instance, for which he had accepted an estimate of £110,500. This continued prodigality at Carlton House caused his downfall, and it was on the understanding that his past debts (by now totalling nearly £500,000) would be cleared and his future income greatly augmented that he agreed to the disastrous marriage with his buxom cousin, Princess Caroline of

The great portico of the Prince Regent's town residence, Carlton House, built by Henry Holland in 1783–95 at enormous expense. The interior delighted Horace Walpole by its 'august simplicity' and 'taste and propriety', while it was lavishly furnished in the latest Greek style, to be known as Regency. The house was demolished in 1826, much of the material being re-used in other royal palaces, and the furniture going to Buckingham Palace and the Royal Pavilion at Brighton.

A chair which was originally part of the furniture of Carlton House and is now at Buckingham Palace.

Brunswick, in 1795.

Here was born their only child, Princess Charlotte, the 'Hope of England', who in May 1816 married Prince Leopold of Saxe-Coburg in the Grand Crimson Drawing Room, and within eighteen months had lost her place in the succession in giving birth to a stillborn son.

In the heyday of the Regency the ballroom at Carlton House became the most fashionable room in England, and the waltz, which great hostesses had banned from their floors as immoral, received Prinney's blessing and became the rage. The wits and beauties of London assembled to play *chemin de fer* in the sanctuary of the Prince's Circular Drawing Room, free from the arm of the law.

The victories over Napoleon were celebrated in 1814 with a series of sumptuous state banquets at Carlton House, attended by the allied sovereigns, statesmen and commanders. The Tsar, the King of Prussia and the lesser German princes, the Russian General Platoff and the bald Prussian Blücher shone with bewildering decorations that Prinney had made it his business to master, and even the shrewd Metternich, the Austrian minister, was impressed by his command of French and German. As a personal celebration of Waterloo he embarked on further alterations to his London house which he entrusted to John Nash, already busily working for him at Brighton and at Regent's Park (as Marylebone Park was henceforth called), where Chester and Cumberland Terraces went forward, but lack of funds delayed work on a grandiose summer palace.

The route of John Nash's Regent Street, sanctioned by Act of Parliament, and sweeping majestically north from the Duke of York's Steps to Langham Place, is London's monument to the Prince Regent, for Carlton House was demolished and the scheme for a great summer palace in Regent's Park evaporated.

With the Regent installed as George IV in new quarters at Windor Castle and Nash's Buckingham Palace going steadily forward, there was no need of Carlton House. All along its upkeep had been a millstone round Prinney's neck and at last he was persuaded to part with it. In September 1826 the Treasury triumphantly informed the Commissioners of Woods and Forests (who were responsible for the fabric and gardens of the royal residences) that His Majesty had 'consented to place His Palace of Carlton House in the hands of the Government for the purpose of selling the materials'. The King's house was to be dismantled. That autumn Sir Thomas Lawrence, P.R.A., called to collect his pictures, and the workmen moved in. Such fixtures as Nash needed at Buckingham Palace and Wyatville at Windsor were carted unceremoniously away. To Windsor went twenty-three chimney-pieces, the parquetting floors of the Ballroom, the Great Drawing-Room and the Circular Drawing-Room and the 'straight floor' from the Gothic Dining Room. The public auction of the remaining fittings and materials brought in comparatively little, though some of the columns of the portico were used at the National Gallery. Carlton Terrace went up in the pleasant gardens but the stables, Carlton Ride, remained for a further thirty years. The gap between the end of Lower Regent Street and the Duke of York's column (erected in 1831) was unfilled. 'The palace' which had embodied the England of the Regency, noted Thackeray with nostalgia, 'exists no more than the palace of Nebuchadnezzar.'

Brighton Pavilion

The development of Brighton as 'England's premier maritime watering-place' was assured when the Duke of Cumberland came to spend the summer of 1779 with Dr. Richard Russell, who had been singing the praises of its healthful air. The Duke was joined for the 1783 season by his nephew, the Prince of Wales, who was so charmed by the place that he decided to find a house for himself near the sea. George was destined to spend more of his life here than anywhere outside the capital, so that Regency Brighton soon eclipsed royal Weymouth.

At first he leased a farm house overlooking the Steine, on the site of the later Pavilion's south drawing room. This far from princely residence, 'no better than a French priest's', he soon replaced by a red brick building designed by Henry Holland. It consisted of a salon, with a domed roof, a music room and a bedroom suite, all furnished in exquisite taste. Here the Prince and Mrs. Fitzherbert entertained the world of fashion, making their stay one long holiday. 'Oh, this wicked Pavilion', wrote Creevey. 'We were there till half-past one this morning and it has kept me in bed with the headache till 12 today.'

At last in 1800 the Prince bought the Pavilion estate and contemplated lavish extensions. William Porder designed for him the stables (modelled on the 'Indian style' of the Hall au Blé, Paris), which have now become the Dome concert hall; next he ordered a little house to be built by the Steine for Mrs. Fitzherbert. Then Humphrey Repton was called in to advise on further schemes and because he had been building Sezincote, Gloucestershire, for an East India Company merchant, his head was stuffed full with Indian ideas. Repton recommended that the Pavilion should be entirely rebuilt according to the principles of Indian architecture and submitted detailed drawings in 1806. Prinney thought them 'perfect', said he would have the work put in hand at once and 'not a tittle shall be altered'. So much for fair words. It was Repton's partner John Nash who began the reconstruction of the Royal Pavilion in

The Banqueting Hall, Brighton Pavilion. Writhing with dragons, it presents a wonderful Chinese extravaganza.

Brighton Pavilion

1815, building first the Banqueting and Music rooms, in a hybrid Oriental style that was not in the slightest 'Indian'.

'To describe its exterior would be a waste of time', wrote a local worthy when George had succeeded to the throne, for everyone who had heard of Brighton had gazed with wonder at woodcuts of the 'domes and airy minarets topped with cupolas and pagoda spires, that distinguish it from anything really English'. For a generation it was reproduced in books and magazines more frequently than any other building in England. Nash's bizarre essay in oriental make-believe was so much of a piece inside and out that it came off. 'The outside is said to be taken from the Kremlin at Moscow', noted Croker on his first visit, and commented a little scathingly 'it seems to me to be copied from its own stables, which perhaps were borrowed from the Kremlin. It is, I think, an absurd waste of money, and will be a ruin in half a century or sooner.'

Three thousand lamps of opalescent glass lit the fairy-tale building. The Entrance Hall set the tone of the building for its walls were painted a Chinese design of pink and green, with various panels depicting dragons. The light from Chinese lanterns picked out strange pagodas and incense-burners, exquisite lacquered cabinets and porcelain figures. The Prince Regent had for some years maintained a 'Chinese Room' at Carlton House as we have seen, but at the new Pavilion he really went to town. There was a Chinese Gallery, fitted out with bamboo furniture, models of junks and eastern trophies. In the Royal Banqueting-Room were two large pictures of scenes from Chinese mythology in imitation of inlaid pearl (they are now to be seen in the Entrance Hall); and its dome was painted to represent an eastern sky. Chinese wallpapers dominated even the Saloon.

The Prince's Chinese phase did not, however, last indefinitely and by the time he had come to the throne as George IV he had thrown overboard the most extravagant features of orientalism for simpler French styles. By then First Empire furniture supplanted bamboo and brass in the drawing-rooms and bedrooms.

The Great Kitchen was, indeed, a show place—'such contrivances for roasting, boiling, baking, stewing, frying, steaming and heating; hot plates, hot closets, hot air, and hot hearths, with all manner of cocks for hot water and cold water, and warm water and steam, and twenty saucepans all ticketed and labelled, placed up to their necks in a vapour bath'. The spits and jacks before the open fireplace were turned by a vane that rotated in the chimney. Here the celebrated Carême presided for eight delicious months as Prinney's chef. (The enormous *batterie de cuisine* on display here today comes from the Duke of Wellington's kitchens at Apsley House).

The Music Room was the most splendid room in the building—'too handsome for Brighton', it was said. The room was 60 feet long and 40 feet wide, with a full dome which improved the acoustics and a magnificent organ. On grand occasions a Turkish band played, but on most evenings there was informal music-making among the guests after dinner.

The Regency Party at Brighton did not really end with George's accession for the Pavilion Estate remained for him the Kingdom that counted, and its coterie was his court. Yet once Nash's work had been finished in every detail, the King lost interest in the place and riveted his attention on the restoration of the royal apartments at

The Great Kitchen at Brighton. Glistening copper utensils (though not the originals— many of them once belonged to the Duke of Wellington) line the walls, a joint roasts on the spit and the tables are laid out in preparation for a banquet.

Brighton Pavilion

Windsor. He did not set foot in Brighton for the last four years of his life.

The Pavilion enjoyed an Indian Summer with William IV, the Sailor King, who regularly spent part of each summer here with Queen Adelaide. His successor, Victoria, was determined on finding a quieter retreat for her family seaside holidays than crowded Brighton and, having settled on Osborne House, she sold the Pavilion to the Brighton Town Commissioners, who soon built a public library and museum in the grounds.

Today the Royal Pavilion contains a permanent Regency Exhibition, and, thanks to the generosity of Her Majesty the Queen and of Queen Mary, much of the original furniture is back in place. The walls have been restored to their original colouring, like the peach blossom pink of the Chinese Corridor. There is no finer collection of *chinoiserie* or of ormolu in England, and few finer exhibits in the world of the characteristic rosewood and mahogany furniture of the Regency period. Although the shade of the First Gentleman pervades the atmosphere of the entire building, two of the rooms on the first floor are maintained as monuments to two other people intimately connected with the Pavilion in its days of greatness. One has been fitted up as the bedroom of Princess Charlotte; the other as Mrs. Fitzherbert's drawing-room. The latter gives an idea of the interior of the Pavilion in its days before the 'Chinese' period. And here on display is Mrs. Fitzherbert's wedding-ring of her secret marriage to the Prince. The final room through which the visitor passes was once the Bath Room. Originally it was lined with marble and held a massive bath, 16 feet long, 10 feet wide and 6 feet deep, into which water was pumped from the sea. For all his patronage of the seaside the Prince Regent never deigned to walk down to the beach, wade in the water and swim.

This detail of the ceiling of the Music Room typifies the richness and the humour of the interior design of Brighton Pavilion.

The happiness of Queen Victoria's first years of marriage were tempered by the distressing fact that the accommodation so royally provided proved utterly unsuitable for a young family. She resented the inconveniences of palace life which involved bringing up her children under the eyes of courtiers and amidst the glare of publicity. After five years of marriage she had four children, yet at Buckingham Palace the nurseries had to be in the attics. The appartments at Windsor were better arranged, but there were no private gardens; while Brighton Pavilion, a possible holiday home, was in the middle of a growing town—'sea air, but no private beach', as the Queen summarily put it. She longed for 'a place of one's own, quiet and retired', such as George III and his consort had enjoyed at Kew, to which her little household could retreat for a period of each year and live informally, much like any other family. To solve her problem she purchased estates at Osborne in the Isle of Wight and at Balmoral in the Scottish Highlands, on each of which new buildings soon arose. Neither estate would have been a practical purchase without the rapid development of the railways.

Victoria recalled with nostalgia her childhood visits to the Isle of Wight and in 1844 asked her Prime Minister, Sir Robert Peel, to make inquiries about suitable property. As a result she took Osborne House, overlooking the Solent, from Lady Isabella Blatchford for a trial year at a rent of £1,000, and she became so enthralled with the setting and real privacy of 'our island home' that in 1845 she purchased the house and some 1,000 acres of woodland and park for £26,000. On her first visit she wrote: 'It is impossible to imagine a prettier spot, valleys and woods which would be beautiful anywhere; but all this near the sea (the woods grow into the sea) is quite perfection; we have a charming beach quite to ourselves. The sea was so blue and calm that the Prince said it was like Naples. And then we can walk about everywhere by ourselves without being followed and mobbed.' Here at last was privacy.

From the beginning the royal couple realized that the existing house would be far too small and a few weeks after purchasing the estate Prince Albert proudly laid the foundation stone of a new Osborne he had designed in collaboration with Thomas

Osborne House

Cubitt, the *avant-garde* builder. Since the Solent resembled the Bay of Naples, they decided upon a Neopolitan villa, with high towers and a loggia on the first floor. By September 1846 the Pavilion wing was ready for the royal family and a Scottish lady-in-waiting maintained tradition by throwing an old shoe after the Queen as she crossed the threshold. The two eastern wings, with quarters for officials and servants, were completed by 1851. Thanks to the sale of Brighton Pavilion and the Prince's economies in running Buckingham Palace, they were able to spend £250,000 on the furnishings of their new home.

There were those who termed the house 'ugly' and even 'vile', yet even these admitted that the setting was superb. The estate gave the Prince Consort the opportunity of indulging in forestry and in laying out gardens, matters on which he was no mean authority. His attempts to 'improve' the grounds at Buckingham Palace and Windsor had been hampered at every turn by the Commissioners of Woods and Forests—'charming departments who really are the plague of one's life', thought the Queen. Much of the old farm lands the Prince planted with oak, beech and elm, but near the house grew such novelties as the Christmas Tree and the Monkey Puzzle Tree which Albert was proud to have introduced to English soil. One of his outdoor schemes was not so successful—the attempt to convert the sewage from the house for use on the gardens; and the Commissioners of Woods and Forests chuckled loud and long.

In the gardens Albert installed a novel 'playroom', direct from Switzerland; and in this 'Swiss Cottage', with its quotations in German carved round the outside, the Princesses learnt the rudiments of domestic science while their brothers were taught how to handle carpenters' tools. They joined forces to help with gardening and each had a personal wheelbarrow and set of tools. Down by the beach was the Queen's own bathing-machine, with its curtained veranda, which ran down a slope into the sea. Both parents hoped that the sight of men-of-war would inculcate in the Prince of Wales their own cherished ideal of his serving in the Royal Navy.

Suddenly in the dreadful December of 1861 the creator of Osborne was no more, and Victoria told her children that the home must remain sacred to their father's memory: the relics they saw around them must never be changed. Here, best of all the Queen could give vent to her private grief and was thankful to have the Solent as a moat between herself and the realities of public life.

As the years went by and Victoria's children in turn married and brought their own offspring to stay for a family seaside holiday, Osborne House was bursting at its seams. The house had no single room that was spacious enough for a large function until in 1891 the 'Durbar Room' was built at the entrance. This Indian hall reflected the Queen's pride in her title of Empress of India; the interior was elaborately decorated by Indian craftsmen under the direction of Bhai Ram Singh, and with its imperial throne at one end the room gave the impression of Oriental splendour. It was lit by electric lamps discreetly concealed in some enormous blue vases which had been presented to the Queen by a group of Indian merchants at the time of the Golden Jubilee. Nothing approaching a 'Durbar' was ever held at Osborne but the room did enable Victoria to entertain all her relations to dinner simultaneously, and provide

Within a year of buying Osborne, work was well advanced on additions to the buildings designed by Thomas Cubitt and Prince Albert in the Italianate style.

a state banquet for crowned heads and other distinguished guests during Cowes Week.

It was at Osborne in the body of her late family that Victoria died, after lingering for two days in January 1901. Years before she had made detailed instructions for the ceremonial to be followed. The widow who had worn nothing but black for forty years had ordered the Dining-Room at Osborne, where she was to lie in state, to be hung in white, her body to be dressed in white, her face covered by her own wedding veil of Honiton lace.

To Edward VII Osborne seemed little less than a mausoleum, for here after forty years were his father's possessions uncannily in place—even a jaunty hat, by now the worse for moth, still hung on its accustomed peg. Happily installed at Sandringham, there was no point in Edward and Alexandra attempting to transform Osborne to meet their exacting tastes. The new King gave most of the estate to the nation, opened the state apartments, with the exception of his mother's private suite, and turned the rest of the house into a convalescent home for officers of the armed forces and civil service. In 1954 Her Majesty the Queen opened her great-great-grandmother's suite to the public. Here the furniture and soft furnishings, the pincushions, china ornaments, family groups and miniatures in their profusion, which set the standard of taste for living-rooms throughout the land, epitomize the spirit of mid-Victorian England.

Balmoral

Glimpses of the Scottish Highlands, made during visits in the royal yacht, so enchanted Victoria that she longed to find a home among the heather, where the mountain air was so invigorating. In 1848, while Osborne was still unfinished, she decided to rent Balmoral House, near Braemar, from the Fife Trustees as an experiment. 'This house is small but pretty', the Queen noted, 'and though the hills seen from the windows are not *so* fine, the scenery all around is the finest almost I have seen anywhere. It is very wild and solitary, and yet cheerful and beautifully wooded.' From the start she dressed the young Princes in tartan kilts, persuaded Albert he must master the steps of reels and soon became 'quite fond of the bagpipes'. Balmoral was for her the most romantic spot in the world.

The house was too small for a growing family and the cabinet minister on duty had to work in a tiny bedroom. The Prince had a billiard table installed in one of the two sitting-rooms but when a game was in progress the Queen had to keep moving from chair to chair to give the players elbow-room. When she purchased the estate in 1852 Albert was already preparing plans for replacing the house by a spacious granite residence. Three years later this was ready for occupation.

With its 100-foot tower and its lesser turrets and gables the new Balmoral appeared as a baronial castle. On every side there was a splendid view—mountains, thick

Balmoral, about which Queen Victoria wrote in her Journal, September 8, 1848: 'It is a pretty little castle in the old Scottish style. There is a picturesque tower and garden in front, with a high wooded hill: at the back is a wood down to the Dee; and the hills rise all around'.

forest, the River Dee. The inside was dominated by pitch-pine and tartan. The Queen had designed the Victoria Tartan and her husband the Balmoral Tartan in red and grey. Fabrics of these patterns, varied by an occasional Royal Stewart, hung at the windows and encased the chairs, while the servants' quarters had tartan linoleum. The Prince had given the closest attention to every detail and made Balmoral as Scottish as the Prince Regent had made Brighton Chinese. When they moved in on September 7, 1855, Victoria was beside herself with joy: 'the house is charming, the rooms delightful, the furniture, papers, everything—perfection'.

Part of the fascination lay in the fact that Balmoral was not, like Osborne, an isolated residence, but the 'big house' of an established community, in which the Queen was determined to play the part of a model laird. She insisted on going out alone when she wanted and calling unannounced at cottages. When she left for London, said one of the villagers, 'it is just like death come all at once'.

She soon came to know all her tenants and remembered perfectly the names of their children and grandchildren and the illnesses they had just recovered from when she had visited them the previous autumn. There was old Miss Grant, 'so tidy and clean', and Kitty Kear, nearly ninety, who went on with her spinning quite unperturbed when the Queen came into her log cabin and said how fast the Princess

Balmoral

Royal was growing. When the Prince of Wales was married at St. George's, Windsor, *all* the Balmoral tenants received invitations.

As a contrast from the estate there were the expeditions on ponies through the wild, exciting country, exploring mountain and glen. Often the royal pair would be accompanied by no more than a lady-in-waiting and a couple of ghillies, and sometimes they travelled *incognito* as 'Lord and Lady Churchill', braving foul weather and putting up with the inconveniences of humble inns.

The children delighted in the open-air activities that the annual visits to Deeside made possible and the highland gathering at Braemar was the most talked-of event in the nursery. The Prince of Wales when seventeen was taken by his father to climb Ben Muich Dhui, the second highest peak in Britain. Before he came of age he was given a home of his own at Birkhall, seven miles away; it was later found to be too small a residence and Abergeldie Castle with its ancient keep, once the home of the Duchess of Kent, was leased to him by the Gordon family whose descendants still lease it to the crown today.

As at Osborne the Prince Consort was for ever busy with plans for the gardens and for his forest at Braemar; to see him so preoccupied made the Queen happy. 'Every year my heart becomes more fixed in this dear Paradise', wrote Victoria, 'and so much more now, that *all* has become my dearest Albert's *own* creation, own work, own building, own laying out, as at Osborne; and his great taste and the impress of his dear hand have been stamped everywhere.'

For the last forty years of her reign the widowed Queen escaped to the seclusion of Balmoral for perhaps five months out of every twelve, for the house in the Highlands kept alive the memory of her husband. She found peace in its solitude, away from what she called 'the mere miserable frivolities and worldliness of this wicked world'. Every room was to be kept as it was in his day, but the house now developed a new routine and a new atmosphere that was quite unlike court life at Windsor or Buckingham Palace. Balmoral was no longer a carefree holiday home and there were strict rules—'like a convent', thought one cabinet minister.

In 1842 when Victoria had made her first railway journey there were comments in the press about her recklessness in taking unnecessary risks. She first travelled by rail from Scotland six years later, when the sea was too stormy for a voyage, and thereafter regularly used the West Coast route on the Great North of Scotland, Caledonian and London and North Western Railways. Her prolonged stays at Balmoral inevitably created difficulties for the prime minister of the day. 'Carrying on the Government of a country 600 miles from the Metropolis doubles the Labour', Disraeli said with feeling, and the cabinet minister in attendance thought himself a prisoner. The household officials intensely disliked John Brown, the rough-tongued ghillie who so fascinated the Queen that she promoted him to be a personal attendant. With his 'warm heart and cheery way of saying things' he could do no wrong in her eyes, even though he was openly rude to her. On his accession Edward VII personally ordered the cairns, monuments and memorial benches, placed in the gardens after his death in 1883, to be removed forthwith.

The ageing Queen could be a trial at times to her children and grandchildren who

Balmoral, of which Queen Victoria wrote in 1856: 'Every year my heart becomes more fixed in this dear Paradise and so much more so now that all has become my dearest Albert's own creation . . . his great taste and the impress of his dear hand have been stamped everywhere'.

were expected to accept invitations to stay at Balmoral with unfeigned eagerness. They sighed and said to each other 'I suppose we had better go'; for though they hated the régime they dared not offend her. Princess May of Teck, who was very much a favourite of Victoria's, found meeting her interrogations terrifying. 'I like Balmoral for about a fortnight', she wrote to her husband in 1895, 'but I honestly think that longer than that is rather an ordeal as the everlasting questions and the carefulness of one's replies is extremely fatiguing in the long run.'

The most that her subjects learnt about Balmoral came from the Queen's two books of extracts from her journals of life in the Highlands. They never knew how bitterly cold the house could be or how tedious the atmosphere.

It was Abergeldie Castle that was still Edward VII's Scottish home, rather than Balmoral, when he came to the throne and although he was proud of wearing his kilt, even in England, he was never really at ease in Deeside. His son, though a great countryman, had his heart at Sandringham and while his visits to Balmoral were as regular though not as prolonged as Queen Victoria's, he had not inherited her personal interest in the place.

A new chapter opened with the accession of George VI. From the very start he was the laird: 'I know so much about this place and I feel I am part of it. I like the people and I believe they like me', he had written. Knowing the estate from his earliest years he had been much disturbed at the hasty changes which Edward VIII had made in the establishment at Balmoral and among the tenants. The new King's interest in the

Balmoral

Balmoral Castle is the private home of the Royal family where the Queen comes in the late summer to enjoy the peace it offers, to ride or walk over her estate, and to picnic in places that were favourite sites to Queen Victoria. Here also Prince Philip enjoys stalking deer or shooting grouse on the rough hills.

estate and its buildings was indeed all-absorbing and the day-to-day problems of a country landowner proved a welcome relief from the business of kingship. Balmoral brought a change of air, the chance of relaxation and the promise of good shooting. He established the autumn visit as an integral part of the royal year and in his closing years, when ill health and fatigue made rest essential, King George admitted that his holidays at Balmoral always made him 'feel a different person'. Balmoral prolonged his life as Bognor had prolonged his father's.

Each August the Royal Family travel north by the royal train or the yacht *Britannia* for their holiday on Deeside. As far as possible it is a holiday for the household staff as well, for they share in the amusements culminating as of old in the ghillies' ball. But since Balmoral remains the private property of the Crown it is maintained, like the Queen Mother's house at neighbouring Birkhall, as a private residence; for instance the names of the guests staying there are not published. As a grand gesture the Queen opens the grounds to the public on occasions and gives the proceeds to hospitals or other deserving causes; crowds gather on late summer days to see the Queen and her family arrive at Crathie Parish Church, but the royal days at Balmoral are not attended by ceremonial functions. When Her Majesty takes part in public affairs it is as laird of Balmoral, presiding at a stall at Crathie Church Fête. Though the interior decorations have changed with the times, in essentials the scene has changed little in a hundred years; the house remains the holiday home that Queen Victoria had set her heart upon.

Frogmore, Queen Charlotte's retreat from Windsor Castle, later the home of the Duchess of Kent, Queen Victoria's mother. In the grounds is the mausoleum built to house the Prince Consort's remains. Queen Victoria often took her breakfast on a summer morning near the lake.

Down the hill from Windsor Castle, towards the river where Eton wetbobs feather their oars, is Frogmore House, still pleasantly rural. The name is not far to seek, for as Queen Victoria observed during a picnic, 'the frogs were quite dreadful, making the grass look as if it were alive'. The property had always been part of the Crown estate and was leased to those high in royal favour; the longest tenancy was that of George Fitzroy, Duke of Northumberland, who was a natural son of Charles II.

When George III became increasingly confined by his malady to Windsor Castle, his consort decided to acquire Frogmore for her own use, for it would enable her to be near at hand without the inconvenience of residing within the Castle. Queen Charlotte bought out the lessee and had the house largely rebuilt by James Wyatt, while the gardens were laid out. After her death the house became the residence of

Sandringham House

her daughter Princess Augusta. When Queen Victoria married she made Frogmore over to her mother, the Duchess of Kent who lived there until her death in March 1861. Victoria, who was at her bedside, called it 'the most dreadful day of my life' and she resolved to leave the house 'just as dear Mama left it—and keep it pretty as it still is'. Before the year was out she was facing an even more terrible loss, with Prince Albert's death and to symbolize her private grief she decided to build at Frogmore a mausoleum. The work was entrusted to Albert Humbert, later to redesign Sandringham, and Professor Ludwig Gruner, who had been the Prince's artistic adviser. Exactly twelve months later all was ready for her three sons—even little Leopold—to help carry their father's coffin to its final resting-place. In search of peace the widowed Queen frequently visited Frogmore and on a summer morning would breakfast in the garden. Forty years on it was in the cruciform mausoleum that she, too, would be buried.

Sandringham House, the Queen's private residence in Norfolk, is the fruit of the Prince Consort's foresight. Albert had invested the revenues of the Duchy of Cornwall from his eldest son's birth so that he would have sufficient funds for buying a property of his own when he came of age and in fact shortly before his death he bought for him the Sandringham Estate from Charles Spencer Cowper, a nephew of Lord Palmerston, for £220,000. A further £60,000 was available for improvements to the

low white house, with its remarkable red-brick conservatory that Samuel Teulon had designed for the sickly Mrs. Harriet Cowper.

After their marriage in 1863 the Prince and Princess of Wales spent as much time as they could in their Norfolk home, and thanks to the development of the railways it was no longer an inaccessible region. At first the house seemed damp and the Prince, fearing his wife's health might suffer, required extensive alterations to be made, provoking a tart comment from his mother: 'Queen Victoria is a disbeliever in the effect of climate on healthy people.' Both Edward and Alexandra enjoyed entertaining, so the original house was soon found to be too small, and was largely replaced by a red-brick mansion in 1870, on the plans of Albert Humbert, who was hampered by his client's insistence that traditional chimneys and gables be retained. A ballroom, library and other features were added piecemeal, so the house seemed unduly rambling, and in the end the only portion of the original building to survive was that incorporated in the billiard room.

The entire house was stamped with the Prince of Wales's personality. His passion for punctuality led to his ordering all the clocks to be kept half an hour fast so that no one could be late. 'Sandringham Time' remained in force until the death of George V; its abolition was the very first act of Edward VIII's reign.

Queen Victoria, who first visited Sandringham when Bertie was seriously ill with typhoid fever in November 1871, wrote her impressions of the house as she came to it by brougham from Wolferton station. 'The road lay between commons and plantations of fir trees, rather wild-looking, flat, bleak country', she noted, and the house 'rather near the high-road, a handsome, quite newly built Elizabethan building.'

It was not only the planning of the great house and its gardens that absorbed the Prince, but the entire estate, which covered six parishes. With obvious pride he told his mother, 'Sandringham improves in appearance every year'. He had a game-keeper's knowledge of every copse and was just as happy in the stables and kennels as in the billiard room; he brought roads to a corner of East Anglia that had for centuries remained off the beaten track, footed large bills for church repairs and took the keenest interest in his tenants' problems. The new cottages on the Sandringham estate which he provided were such model dwellings that the Liberal government in 1884 appointed the Prince a member of the Royal Commission on the Housing of the Working Classes.

A few hundred yards from the big house a cottage had been built as an annex by Albert Humbert in gabled Victorian Gothic, with stone walls and a slate roof, and in 1893 the Prince settled it on his son, George, Duke of York. York Cottage, as it was now called, down by the lake, half-hidden by laurels and thick clumps of rhododendrons, was not just the honeymoon cottage to which the Duke brought Princess May; it was to be their permanent home for thirty-three years. With its imitation Tudor beams and stained-glass fanlights it might have been the suburban villa of a not very successful solicitor. It seems fantastic that room could be found in this 'undesirable little villa' for a family of eight, with nannies and tutors, lords and ladies-in-waiting, domestic and secretarial staff and guests. Apart from the principal bedroom the upstairs rooms were little more than cubicles. Where everybody managed to sleep

Sandringham House, as drawn by architect Albert Humbert in about 1865, showing a building which is a convincing reproduction of a Jacobean country house.

Sandringham House

remained a mystery even to the Duke of York: he supposed, he once said, that the servants must sleep in the trees. The oddest room in York Cottage was his own sitting-room, on the north side. The cheerless outlook on to dense shrubberies was not improved by the interior decoration; instead of paper its walls were covered with scarlet cloth of the type 'used in those days for the trousers of the French army'. In the cottage the six York children spent most of their childhood and here all but the eldest was born.

George V always spoke of 'Dear old Sandringham, the place I love better than anywhere in the world', yet he lived in the big house for no more than ten years. Queen Alexandra stayed on as mistress of the house she helped to plan until her death in 1925, to the very end discussing improvements to the gardens with her controller,

(Left). *The imposing porch of Sandringham House, and* (above) *the house which George V, described as 'the place I love better than anywhere in the world'.*

Sandringham House

Sandringham House from the air—the private estate which has been the much loved home of the royal family for a hundred years. Edward VII, as Prince of Wales, was devoted to it. George V died at Sandringham, while George VI was born and died there. The latter had inherited his father's love of the house and hoped his daughter, the future Queen Elizabeth, would hold it in the same affection: 'I want Lilibet and Philip to get to know it too as I have always been so happy here and I love the place', he wrote to Queen Mary, and when Prince Charles, as a little boy, was staying with his grandparents at Sandringham King George wrote to Princess Elizabeth, 'He is the fifth generation to live there and I hope he will get to love the place.'

old Sir Dighton Probyn, as her husband had done down to the last weeks of his life.

It was from a tiny room under the staircase that George made his first Christmas Day broadcast in 1932. At Sandringham, appropriately, he was to end his days.

Edward VIII remained content with Fort Belvedere, on the edge of Windsor Great Park and regarded Sandringham as the bastion from which his father had waged his 'private war with the twentieth century'. Yet he asked his brother, the Duke of York, to make a survey of the estate and suggest reforms. In the event, with the Duke's succession to the throne within eleven months, Sandringham had another squire. George VI was a countryman with a profound understanding of wild life and his re-organization of the shooting on the estate embodied a code of sportsmanship in which cruelty and intolerance had no place. After the long interval of war, he was delighted to return to Sandringham in 1945. He was out shooting on the day before he died, wearing a specially-heated jacket, and with his last three cartridges cleanly shot three hares.

Sandringham remains for the present Queen what it has been all along: a private house, away from formal occasions and the pressures of court life, to which the royal family can retreat for holidays, even though the dispatch-boxes are never far away. Her Majesty opens the grounds periodically for the benefit of local charities and television cameras have even penetrated the library, on the site of Edward VII's American bowling alley.